KUNG FU
BASICS

KUNG FU
BASICS

Paul Eng

TUTTLE Publishing

Tokyo | Rutland, Vermont | Singapore

Published by Tuttle Publishing, an imprint of Periplus Editions (HK) Ltd.

Library of Congress Cataloging-in-Publication Data

Eng, Paul.
   Kung fu basics / Paul Eng ; calligraphy by Paul Eng ; photographs by David Taran ; illustrations by Don Hopkins. — 1st ed.
       190 p. : ill., 25 cm
   ISBN 0-8048-3494-6 (pbk)
1. Kung fu. I. Title: Kung fu basics. II. Title. GV1114.7.E53 2004
796.815'9—dc22

                                                  2003027773

ISBN-13: 978-0-8048-4702-5
(Previously published as ISBN 978-0-8048-3494-0)

Distributed by:
North America, Latin America,
and Europe
Tuttle Publishing
364 Innovation Drive
North Clarendon, VT 05759-9436
Tel: (802) 773-8930;Fax: (802) 773-6993
info@tuttlepublishing.com
www.tuttlepublishing.com

Japan
Tuttle Publishing
Yaekari Building, 3rd Floor
5-4-12 O–saki, Shinagawa-ku
Tokyo 141-0032
Tel: (03) 5437-0171;Fax: (03) 5437-0755
sales@tuttle.co.jp
www.tuttle.co.jp

Asia Pacific
Berkeley Books Pte. Ltd.
61 Tai Seng Avenue #02-12
Singapore 534167
Tel: (65) 6280-3320; Fax: (65) 6280-6290
inquiries@periplus.com.sg
www.periplus.com.sg

First edition
21 20 19 18   6 5 4 3 2 1   1801MP
Printed in Singapore

TUTTLE PUBLISHING® is a registered trademark of Tuttle Publishing, a division of Periplus Editions (HK) Ltd.

Acknowledgments

Special thanks to David Taran, Don Hopkins, and Martha Dahlen for their generous help.

table of contents

Part 4: *Practice* 103

Part 5: *Making Progress* 157

WHAT IS KUNG FU? Kung fu is a living tradition of Chinese martial arts that has been passed down from generation to generation of dedicated practitioners, for more than 1,400 years.

It is the application of a science of body mechanics and energy dynamics. Its drills, movements, techniques, and forms are the application of a deep understanding of how the body works, how power is generated, how energy is transformed—and of how fitness and longevity can be achieved.

It is a way of life and a way of fighting, a method for total self-development, as well as a collection of effective combat techniques.

It is Chinese. It is inextricably bound with elements of Chinese culture and philosophy, with Taoism, Confucianism, and Buddhism, as well as with ancient legends, modern heroes, and age-old traditions.

It is both sport and art. Learning kung fu means undertaking rigorous training to learn specific stances, hand techniques, and footwork, while doing kung fu is essentially artistic expression. Beauty and grace are as important as speed and power.

Kung fu is also a community. It is a family of dedicated practitioners who share a love of kung fu and who have committed themselves to one another, to the teachers before them, and to the art and its preservation.

The purpose of this book is to help a new student get started. The chapters of this book are organized roughly in the sequence of a beginner's experience—from choosing the school, through training, to participating in tournaments. It is meant to cover the material taught in approximately the first three to six months of training, with hints of what comes beyond. We start with history because that explains how the different styles developed and with philosophy because that explains what the art is trying to teach.

We have tried to be complete and accurate, but words can only capture the shadow of the reality. As it is written in the *Tao Te Ching*, "The Tao that can be described is never the true Tao," so it is with kung fu: that which you experience is the true essence, and that essence is far richer than words can describe. Good luck!

Jing: Most commonly translated as simply "respect," this word also includes the ideas of admiration, courtesy, awe, surprise, astonishment, and discipline. With this kind of attitude, a beginner is mentally ready to learn.

part 1
introduction

chapter 1
history of kung fu

THERE ARE TWO HISTORIES of kung fu. One is the history of the name, and the other is the history of the martial arts that it represents. For most of China's history, the two characters pronounced "kung fu" meant the application of determined perseverance to accomplish some task. It could be used to describe any work at all—house-work, schoolwork, practice, or job. Toward the end of the nineteenth century, people in the southern provinces (particularly Canton) adopted "kung fu" as a slang term for martial artists because they practiced so hard. When movies came out featuring these fighting artists, the term was applied to the discipline as a whole. And it stuck because it was a useful way of distinguishing the tra-ditional fighting arts from the version being created in Mainland China for performance and competition (*wushu*), even though "wushu" is actually the older name and a more accurate translation for the term "martial art."

Figure 1-1: Small section of a mural in one of the halls of the Shaolin Temple in Henan Province

Semantics aside, the martial arts—by whatever name—are an integral part of Chinese culture and civilization. They have developed, as the civilization has, in accordance with the social, political, and technological forces of the Asian continent for more than 4,000 years.

The earliest roots of the martial arts are in the combat sports of the Han civilization along the Yellow River. But very quickly these sports also became sources of entertainment and health exercises, and the balance between military and "folk" wushu has varied over the centuries. In times of peace interest in the martial aspects waned, and soldiers left their profession, some joining acrobatic or operatic troupes or performing in the streets. During times of political upheaval, interest in the martial arts rebounded, as even farmers needed to defend themselves from bandits and outlaws.

The four major historical phases of the Chinese martial arts:

I. Ancient age of combat and entertainment

II. Age of northern Shaolin

III. Age of dispersion

IV. Modern age of kung fu and wushu

Buddhism, Taoism, and Confucianism are important components of wushu philosophy, and its connection with Buddhism has been pivotal. When Bodhidharma taught the Shaolin monks health-preserving exercises, he not only approved physical health as a necessary part of spiritual practice, but also irrevocably linked the two and established a location (the temple) to centralize the teaching, preservation, and advancement of these integrated wushu/kung fu techniques. Later, when the Manchus sacked and burned the temple, the monks and their fighting techniques were scattered, which led to the development of myriad styles of kung fu throughout Southeast Asia.

Finally, in the twentieth century, when firearms ended the military usefulness of wushu, its grace, beauty, health-giving benefits, and cultural heritage ensured its survival in China as modern "wushu" and in countries elsewhere as "kung fu."

Very roughly, the history of the Chinese martial arts can be divided into four major phases: The age of ancient military arts and entertainment, the age of northern Shaolin, the age of dispersion; and the modern age of kung fu and wushu. The notes below record the milestones of these phases.

Phase I: The Age of Ancient Military Arts and Entertainment

Shang Dynasty (c. 1600–1000 B.C.)

The first reliable records of kung fu, both external and internal forms, are made on oracle bones and turtle shells. Combat sports are primarily exercises for military preparation and include both wrestling (unarmed) and combat with weapons. Later in the dynasty, government schools are established to train soldiers.

Western Chou Dynasty (c. 1000–770 B.C.)

Wrestling, archery, chariot racing, and swordplay are popular; fighting methods are performed as dances accompanied by music.

Spring and Autumn Period (770–475 B.C.)

The martial arts, known as *chuan yung*, flourish. Swords are used in warfare for the first time. In 512 Sun Tzu writes a treatise on military strategy, *The Art of War*.

Confucius encourages his disciples to learn both literary and martial arts. Lao-tzu, legendary author of the *Tao Te Ching*, the classic Taoist gospel, lives in the sixth century B.C. In India, Buddha is teaching (c. 560–483 B.C.).

Warring States Period (475–221 B.C.)

Ch'in Dynasty (221–207 B.C.)

After centuries of war the Ch'in emerge victorious, unify China, and give it its name. Emperor Shih Huang-ti (who ordered the terra-cotta armies made for his tomb in Xian) undertakes grand projects, including the unfication of the Great Wall and the standardization of script, coinage, weights, and measures.

Western and Eastern Han Dynasties (206 B.C.–A.D. 200)

The Old Silk Road opens; trade with Rome southern and western Asia flourish. Paper is invented. First Buddhist missionaries reach China from India, c. A.D. 65

Hua Tuo, a renowned medical doctor considered to be the father of acupuncture, creates the Five Animal Exercises (*Wu Chien Shi*)—based on the characteristics of the deer, bird, monkey, tiger, and bear. Supposedly Taoist in origin, these revolutionary exercises will influence many martial arts styles and health exercises and will become integral to the Shaolin martial arts system.

Phase II: The Age of Northern Shaolin

Six Dynasties (220–589)

During the Three Kingdoms period (c. 220–265), three rival states contest fiercely, spawning many legendary heroes and tales to be recorded later in the classic novel *Romance of the Three Kingdoms*.

In 495 a Buddhist temple is built on Mt. Songshan near Luoyang in Henan Province and named Shaolin.

The single most influential figure in the history of China's martial arts was the Buddhist monk Bodhidharma.

In 520 the monk Da Mo (Bodhidharma) arrives to teach the *Chan* (Zen) practice of Buddhism at the Shaolin Temple. Finding that the monks lack the physical stamina to meditate effectively, he develops exercises to strengthen them, namely, the "Eighteen Buddha Hands."

Two famous classics, of which there are no surviving copies, are written: the *Sinew-Changing Classic* (*Yi Jin Jing*) and the *Washing Marrow Classic* (*Xi Sui Jing*). Some attribute these classics to Bodhidharma. Due to the health benefits and Buddhist influence, from this time on the martial arts are widely practiced by citizens, not just by the nobility and military professionals.

For the first time Chinese martial arts spread outside China when soldiers sent to Korea teach there.

Tang Dynasty (618–906)

In this warring period intense persecution of Buddhists batters the monasteries. Gunpowder is introduced, changing forever the nature of war and fighting.

A court examination system is initiated, and all officers and soldiers must pass martial arts tests for recruitment and promotion.

Northern and Southern Song Dynasties (960–1279)

During this period of relative social and political stability, both military sports and "folk" wushu flourish. The first emperor, Song Tai Zu, creates a long fist style (*Tai Zu Chang Quan*), which will be called the grandfather of present kung fu styles. General Yue Fei converts a spear form into a hand form and then into *xingyiquan* ("mind and intention" boxing), which is the beginning of soft or internal styles. He also teaches an external style, which becomes the basis of eagle claw styles.

After 1126 martial arts spread south of the Yangtze and west, even into Thailand.

In 1224 Pai Yu-feng joins the Shaolin Temple. Appalled at finding both the spirit and artistry of the monks in serious decline, he expands the Eighteen Buddha Hands to the 128 Buddha Hands and divides it into the five fist system: dragon, tiger, snake, leopard, crane. Each animal represents a different quality that should be developed to maintain overall health. This system epitomizes the fundamentals of Shaolin kung fu and survives today, particularly in forms of the *Hung Gar* style.

Yuan Dynasty (1271–1368)

Mongols from the north under Kublai Khan conquer northern China. Marco Polo visits (1275–1292).

The Yuan rulers encourage their own people to practice martial arts but forbid the Han from practicing or keeping weapons. Operatic troupes flourish, and more than 300 scripts are written, many featuring fighting scenes using weapons as props. Hence the level of wushu technique improves, and the martial virtues (fighting injustice, eliminating evil) spread. Five more Shaolin temples are established in various parts of northern China.

Arabian and Persian Moslems move to China and adopt the martial arts exercises. They will continue to practice, develop, spread, and preserve the martial arts, even up to the present.

Ming Dynasty (1268–1644)

The Golden Age of Chinese Martial Arts. Schools flourish, and training is widespread and vigorous. A Shaolin temple is established in Fukien Province in southern China. Wang Long of Shantung creates the famous Praying Mantis Style.

In 1387 *Romance of the Three Kingdoms*, the oldest surviving novel in the world, and *Outlaws of the Marsh* are published. Both recount heroic tales of legendary martial arts masters. In particular, *Outlaws* has many scenes of wushu, providing an accurate glimpse into the state of the martial arts at the time. Subsequently many books on wushu technique and strategy appear.

Toward the end of the dynasty, Cheng Yuanyun goes to Japan to teach *chin-na* and Chinese wrestling; from these roots *jujitsu* develops.

Phase III: The Age of Dispersion
Ching Dynasty (1644–1911)

The Ming dynasty comes to an abrupt and violent end when Manchurian troops storm the capital, Beijing. Fierce hatred between the Han and the Manchurian intruders means a constant threat of rebellion and constant efforts to root out Ming loyalists. During the 1800s, thousands of Chinese emigrate to the United States, seeking work and establishing communities ("Chinatowns") where Chinese cultural traditions, including the martial arts, thrive.

In 1700 Manchurians burn the Shaolin Temple in Henan, as a potential haven for rebels; the monks disperse, and the development of the martial arts will never again be centralized. Some monks move south, teaching and developing the art privately. Some migrate to other parts of Southeast Asia.

In 1901 military exams are discarded; "folk" wushu becomes the principal practice for health, sport, and entertainment.

Especially toward the end of the dynasty, secret societies become active, practicing martial arts for rebellion; foreigners call them "Boxers." Some societies teach their members that their kung fu will protect them from bullets, which is proven tragically false in the Boxer Rebellion of 1911.

Phase IV: Modern Age of Kung fu and Wushu
Republic (1912–1949)

Political turmoil erupts. In 1912, led by Sun Yat-sen, the Republic of China is founded; in 1921 the Chinese Communist Party forms, opposing Chiang Kai-shek's Kuomintang party. Japanese occupy China (1937–1945).

At the turn of the twentieth century, popular opinion is strongly divided as to whether China should preserve its heritage of martial arts or adopt Western competitive sports. (Well-educated Chinese disdain exercise in any form.) Ultimately, both are encouraged. Chinese martial arts are referred to by their historical name, wushu, meaning "martial" (*wu*) "arts" (*shu*). In 1928 the Central Wushu Institute is established. In 1936 a Chinese wushu team performs at the Berlin Olympics.

People's Republic (1949–present)

In 1949 the Chinese Communist Party, led by Mao Tse-tung, establishes the People's Republic of China. Hong Kong, while geographically and culturally a part of Canton Province, remains politically a part of Britain. The capitalistic economy supports independence from China in many areas, including the martial arts.

On the Mainland
1956: The Chinese Wushu Association is set up.

1958: The State Physical Culture and Sports Commission defines exercise routines and competition rules for various styles of wushu.

1966–76: During the Cultural Revolution, wushu is discouraged as a feudal practice; many martial artists escape to Hong Kong, where their arts are filmed and marketed as "kung fu movies."

1982: The First National Wushu Conference establishes general and specific policies for the development of wushu. The emphasis is on demonstration, performance, and competition, rather than martial arts applications. Subsequently, wushu associations, clubs, centers, and societies are set up in all parts of the country.

1985: The First International Wushu Invitational Tournament is held. It has been held annually ever since.

1990: The International Wushu Federation is formally established; wushu is included as an official competition event at the Asian Games.

In Hong Kong
1972: The movie *Fists of Fury*, starring Bruce Lee, opens in Hong Kong, grossing millions on its first day. The Hong Kong film industry is already making millions on this new genre, termed "kung fu movies" after the local slang term for the martial arts.

1973: In the U.S. David Carradine stars in the weekly drama *Kung Fu*, which presents not only the dramatic aspects of Chinese martial arts, but also moral and cultural aspects, thus winning the respect of a wider audience.

1970s: Enrollment in kung fu classes mushrooms in schools in the U.S., particularly in big cities; Chinese martial arts are widely taught to non-Asians for the first time.

Today, in addition to both wushu and the many styles of kung fu, other martial arts of Asia are being taught all over the world, and new styles and forms are being created, particularly for self-defense.

chapter 2
philosophy

THE STUDY AND PRACTICE of kung fu has always had strong spiritual, moral, and ethical components. Why? How did it become more than a collection of fighting techniques? The reasons have to do with the influences of Buddhism, Taoism, and Confucianism in the context of Chinese culture. Although today the ethical elements of kung fu have been somewhat obscured by mass marketing and commercialism—that is, by the need of kung fu masters and schools to survive in a commercial world—nevertheless, they do survive and perhaps explain kung fu's continuing appeal to modern generations, both Eastern and Western. Understanding the three strongest philosophical roots of kung fu will give a profound and essential dimension to your practice.

Buddhism

The Buddha was a man who found a way to reduce personal suffering through self-awareness. He emphasized that the only way to achieve true, enduring happiness was through one's own concentrated effort, and he summarized how one should work toward this goal in his "eightfold path," which is: right understanding, right aspirations, right action, right speech, right livelihood, right effort, right concentration, and right mindfulness. Thus, the life Buddha encouraged his followers to lead was not a passive one, but rather one in which every thought and deed was focused in one direction: toward eliminating suffering. In the course of his own search, Buddha found that stringent ascetic practices—punishing the physical body—did not bring him closer to enlightenment. Indeed, on the contrary, a healthy physical body enhanced spiritual practices, enabling longer and more focused meditation. This explains the first introduction of physical exercises in the Shaolin Temple; it perhaps also explains why, traditionally, masters of the Chinese martial arts have also been masters of the healing arts.

Buddha's Eightfold Path

Right understanding

Right aspirations

Right action

Right speech

Right livelihood

Right effort

Right concentration

Right mindfulness

Buddha's teaching of compassion translates into nonviolence and the use of power only as a last resort. Thus, from Buddhism, came the understanding that violence could not end violence and that any action done in anger can only create more anger. Real victory, the Buddhist scriptures suggest, lies in eliminating animosity and hatred. If you can transform and/or eliminate your opponent's desire to fight, then you achieve ultimate self-defense.

Taoism

Taoism, or the philosophy of the *Tao,* is expressed most famously in the *Tao Te Ching,* or *Dao De Jing,* a collection of terse, enigmatic observations on nature, ostensibly written by the philosopher Lao-tzu in the sixth century B.C. Taoism teaches that the entire universe is animated by a vital energy that can be felt and only roughly defined in words as the "Tao." Any movement in harmony with nature, or with the Tao, flows freely, without resistance. Thus, human happiness, peace, contentment, success, and immortality all lie in coming into perfect harmony with the Tao of nature. By eliminating the fears, desires, and judgment of personal ego, you will, in some sense, be carried away by the Tao—"acting without intention" and "winning without a fight."

When Taoist martial artists looked to nature, they came away influenced in three specific and very important ways. First, the masters modeled their fighting techniques on wild animals, such as the tiger, monkey, and praying mantis. Second, the paradox of the power of softness, yielding, and submissiveness influenced many of their approaches to strategy in fighting. That is, there was and is much emphasis on sensing your opponent's intention, receiving the power of a punch or kick "submissively," and then turning that power—your opponent's own strength—against him or her. Developing sensitivity and intuitive understanding of an opponent is a critical part of martial arts study and practice. Finally, in their study of the subtle energy of the universal Tao, the Taoist martial artists also developed understanding of human internal energy and the means to cultivate, circulate, and use it, as applied in the "soft" or internal aspects of the martial arts.

Taoist influence on the Martial Arts

☞ Use of wild animals as models

☞ Paradox of the power of the soft

☞ Cultivation of personal energy

Confucianism

Confucius, who lived at about the same time as Lao-tzu, focused his life and philosophy on how to achieve harmony in society. He believed that the key was maintaining appropriate relationships between people, beginning with the core relationships of a family between father and son and husband and wife. If these relationships were strong, then stability and harmony would resonate throughout the nation—to all on earth under heaven. The eight basic virtues he taught were: loyalty, trust, filial piety, responsibility for those under you, courtesy, honor, humility, and sense of personal shame.

From Confucius, then, comes the strong family structure of kung fu societies: the loyalty to fellow martial artists within your organization and the reverence for present teachers and past generations of masters. From his teachings, also, perhaps comes the respect for the art itself, as a living entity that students must honor, cherish, and perpetuate. This strong moral structure has carried the secrets of the Chinese martial arts through generations, helping to ensure their survival better than if their principles had been written down.

Eight Virtues of Confucius

Loyalty

Trust

Filial piety

Responsibility for those under you

Courtesy

Honor

Humility

Sense of personal shame

忠 信 孝 悌 禮 義 廉 恥

The "patron saint" of the martial arts, Guan Gung, or Guan Dai or Guan Ti, is also considered a god of justice. In the past, schools of martial arts invariably had a shrine dedicated to him with a picture or statue. He is typically depicted dressed half in the clothes of a soldier and half in the robes of a scholar.

Ethics

Over the centuries, Buddhism, Taoism, and Confucianism have provided a moral and ethical context to the Chinese martial arts that is not only integral to their practice but also to their survival. Today, while each kung fu style and school may have its own particular code of ethics, the basic principles are universal, and may be summarized as follows.

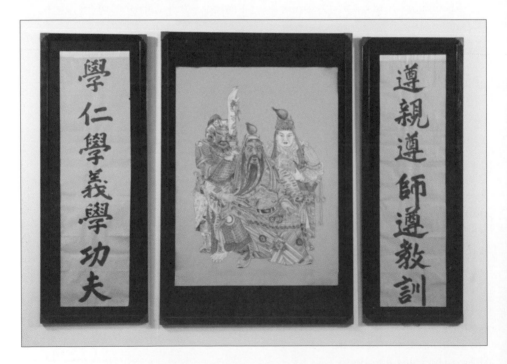

Figure 2-1: Typical display in a traditional kung fu school. Patron saint Guan Ti is in the center with his adopted son Guan Ping (right) and sword-bearer Zhou Cang (left). The words on the right read "Obey parents, obey teachers, obey the teachings." The words on the left read, "Learn kindness, learn honor, learn kung fu."

Attitude toward Others

Respect:

For human life and society

For all martial arts and martial artists

For the teachings received

For teachers

For fellow students

Compassion

Courtesy

Loyalty

Trustworthiness

Devotion, honor, and respect to one's parents

Sense of responsibility for those under you

Personal Qualities

Humility/Modesty

Honesty

Diligence

Patience

Enthusiasm

Self-control

Techniques learned are to be used only as a last resort and in defense.

KUNG FU COMES in a range of styles, from the vigorous and acrobatic to the subtle and elegant. After hundreds of years of history and development all over the continent of Asia, this is not surprising. The notes in this chapter first list styles of Asian martial arts which are *not* kung fu (in case there is any doubt) and then attempt to give a general overview of martial arts in China and of the kung fu styles most widely available in schools outside of Asia.

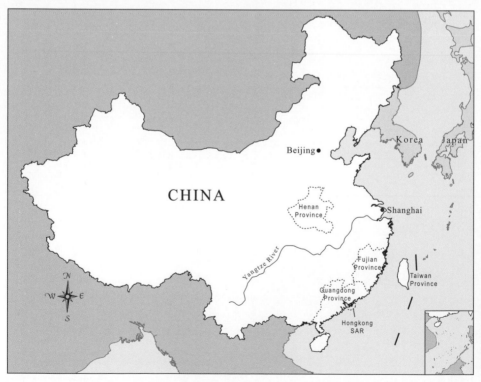

Figure 3-1: Map of China

Asian Martial Arts Outside China

Korea: taekwondo, *Farang Do, Tang Soo Do, Hapkido*

Japan: aikido, judo, jujitsu, karate (*Gojiu, Yamakochi, Shaodikan*); *Kempo* (*Kenpo*)

Thailand: *Muay Thai (Mui Thay)*

Chinese Martial Arts

The Chinese martial arts are categorized in different ways.

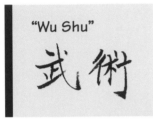

"Wu Shu"

"Kung Fu"

Kung fu vs. Wushu

One distinction that should be clarified at the start is the difference between kung fu and wushu. "Wushu" is the pronunciation of the Chinese characters that mean "martial arts"; that is, "wu" means "martial or military, having to do with fighting," while "shu" means "arts." This is now a specific term that refers to the Chinese government's officially approved version of the traditional martial arts. Organized and codified by committees in the last twenty years, wushu is primarily for competition and demonstration. Therefore, its forms, while derived from traditional models, now include many gymnastic and acrobatic forms to make them more appealing in performance before an audience.

In contrast, "kung fu" is the pronunciation of the Chinese characters that mean "dedicated work." This was a colloquial term that became popular in Canton Province during the nineteenth century, to refer to people who studied the martial arts, because they worked so hard. When the Hong Kong film

Which Style Is for Me?

The new student should read these notes for information, but not necessarily for guidance in choosing a style to study. Especially at the beginning, the quality of the school and the teacher could be more important than choice of style.

See Chapter 4 for more discussion of this dilemma.

industry began producing movies using these arts, they were called "kung fu movies." As a result, today "kung fu" identifies and refers to the traditional fighting techniques and forms as handed down through centuries of teaching and generations of practitioners.

Internal or Soft vs. External or Hard

Both systems and styles of the Chinese martial arts are often described or categorized as being "internal/soft" or "external/hard," where "internal" refers to subtle, inner power and "external" refers to obvious, physical movements. This distinction is most apparent only at the first level of learning because all categories have both internal and external elements. So-called "internal" forms generally begin with developing internal energy (relaxed movements, mental focusing, breathing, and the like) and later express it externally, while so-called "external forms" begin with developing external power (punches, blocks, kicks, and so on) and later work on the internal. To truly master any style, you must develop both aspects. It's just a question of how you start.

"Tai Chi Chuan"

"Qigong"

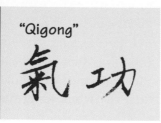

Tai Chi Chuan, Qigong, and Kung fu/Wushu

Tai chi chuan (or taijiquan), qigong, and kung fu/wushu are modern labels for different systems within the Chinese martial arts. Before the twentieth century there were no distinctions, and anyone studying the martial arts learned all three. Tai chi chuan is a slow, meditative exercise, considered to develop internal power first. It is basically a kung fu/wushu form done in slow motion. Qigong means "breathing or energy exercise"; it comprises externally simple, repetitive exercises that use mind and breath control to develop the *qi,* or internal vital energy. Compared to qigong and tai chi chuan, kung fu is considered an external system, because it requires complex and intense physical training and is mostly expressed in visible physical movements. In most styles of kung fu, the internal training comes later after the external forms have been mastered. Some kung fu styles are considered more "internal" than others, although all contain both elements. It is the mastery of both aspects that takes a lifetime of practice.

Kung fu Categories

Traditional Chinese martial arts tend to fall into two broad groups based on geography—north and south of the Yangtse River. Centuries ago, northern wheat-eating people tended to be large in stature; they often rode horses (which requires strong legs) and were used to wide-open spaces. Thus, corresponding to body type, northern styles of kung fu generally emphasize power and kicks. In contrast, southern, rice-eating people tended to be smaller and to live and fight in smaller spaces; many were fisherfolk, used to balancing in boats. Thus, southern styles generally emphasize agility and punches and hand and arm techniques. (A traditional martial arts saying summarizes this as, "*Nam quan bei tui*," or "Southern hands, northern legs.") In addition, historically, most of the southern styles developed in the seventeenth century among rebels seeking to overthrow the Ching dynasty. Thus, these styles developed more quickly than the northern styles and tended to teach hard power first, and internal power later in order to meet the needs of the times.

Below are listed some of the most common kung fu styles that are widely taught outside of Asia.

Northern Styles

Chang Quan ("Long Fist")

This is considered the original kung fu system, created during the Song dynasty (c. A.D. 960) and now broadened to include many forms. It is considered excellent for general health and as a foundation for learning weapons forms later. Because of its graceful forms, it is also popular for competitions. Adapted forms are included in the modern wushu repertory.

Northern Praying Mantis

Another old style, originating at the end of the Ming dynasty, Northern Praying Mantis is a comprehensive style with many forms suitable for all body types and all speeds. It is reputedly one of the potentially most fierce styles, with distinctive hand movements (like the praying mantis) and quick footwork. Among the branches of this style are: Seven Star, Six Harmony, Plum Blossom, and Tai Chi Praying Mantis.

Monkey

This style is based on the typical movements and innate nature of a monkey. Forms involve a lot of acrobatics (tumbling, rolling), unpredictable movements, and low stances.

Eagle Claw

Founded around A.D. 1200, this style resembles jujitsu in its speed and its emphasis on joint locks and use of pressure points to catch and control, rather than to kill or maim. For these reasons, it is useful for police work that involves disarming criminals and for self-defense for women. Even so, this style is seldom taught because it is so potentially powerful.

Xingyiquan (Hsing-I)

This style originated between the years 960 and 1279, and is now considered one of the highest levels of internal kung fu. The style employs simple techniques (direct strikes, secure footwork) with the aim of ending conflict as quickly as possible. Derived from theories of the Five Elements and Twelve Animals, the forms seek to train internal energy as the source of external power.

Bagua (Pa Kwa, "Eight Trigrams")

This style, too, has a reputation for training internal energy and is perhaps the most atypical of the kung fu systems. Students training in *Bagua* walk a circle, rather than using training stances; learning the eight directions of the circle teaches flexibility and how to use the whole body as a weapon.

Southern Styles

Hung Gar ("Hung Family Style")

Hung Gar was, and still is, one of the most famous and popular Southern systems. It is good for all ages and all body structures. While it is considered by some to be relatively slow, it is powerful. It includes isometric and dynamic tension exercises that not only develop strong arms and legs, but also generate considerable internal power.

Choi Lee Fut (Choy Lee Fut)

A relatively new system, developed in the early nineteenth century, *Choi Lee Fut* has become one of the most popular in Southeast Asia. It includes a wide range of hand, weapon, and wooden dummy forms and is reportedly one of the most powerful in application.

Wing Chun (Wing Tsun)

Like Hung Gar, *Wing Chun* was created in the late seventeenth century by rebels seeking to overthrow the Ching dynasty. (Tradition holds that Wing Chun was created by a woman, but this story seems to be one of the ploys to protect the true creator and his followers, rather than the truth.) With only three hand forms, one wooden dummy set, and a few weapons forms, the Wing Chun style is simple, economical in terms of movement, and aggressive. Many consider it a good choice of styles for those seeking to learn self-defense techniques quickly.

Modern Style
Jeet Kune Do (JKD)

The only style developed in the twentieth century, *Jeet Kune Do* is Bruce Lee's creation. After winning a fight with Wing Chun techniques, but judging his performance a failure (Lee felt he should have won faster, with less effort), Lee created JKD, which translates as "the way of the intercepting fist." JKD tends to use kicking techniques, as in northern styles, with hand techniques from the south. While it incorporates many Wing Chun principles, it is even more direct and efficient, with an emphasis on self-awareness and intention. There are no forms to learn in this style; training is in techniques and application.

part 2
getting started

THE FOUR CHAPTERS in this section will guide you up through your first class. While this part of your new relationship with kung fu will be short, it is important. Knowing what to expect of the teacher and other students, and what they will be expecting from you, will help you start out with the right attitude and that in turn will ensure you settle quickly into training.

The first step is to choose a school. From there, a great deal of the rest follows: what to wear, how to behave, how to participate in classes. While much is specific to a given school, much is also universal, and this is what we try to present in the following chapters.

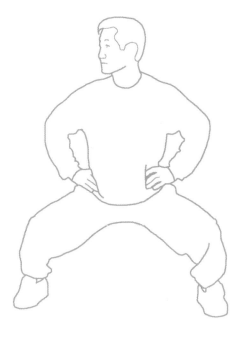

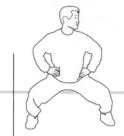

chapter 4
choosing the
right school

I F YOU TRAIN IN KUNG FU seriously—which means two or three, or even more, workouts per week—your school will begin to seem like a second home. Therefore, consider carefully before you make a commitment. What's available in your area will certainly limit your choice, but do your best to match your goals and personal preferences with the style of school—and particularly the instructor—that you choose. This is an important first step toward satisfaction and progress in your studies.

Personal Goals

Begin by asking yourself why you want to study kung fu. What do you want to get out of it? What do you want to achieve? Five common reasons are described below with comments as to how this would influence your choice of a school.

First, and perhaps most obviously, people take up a martial art because they want to participate in a combat sport. They like to spar, as in wrestling or boxing; they want to learn theory and strategy as well as effective techniques. People with this goal in mind should be sure there is plenty of sparring at the school they choose and that the teacher (*sifu*) is well versed in the applications of the moves of the forms taught. In this case, a traditional kung fu school is likely to be more suitable than wushu (which is more focused on performance, see below).

A second reason for studying kung fu, closely related to the first, is self-defense. Again, some schools emphasize these aspects with many free-sparring sessions and careful demonstrations of the applications of the moves in the practice forms. Those concerned about self-defense should be sure the school they join can provide this training.

Third, many people take up a martial art for physical fitness. You may mainly want to "keep fit," to lose weight, tone muscle, or simply stay healthy. If so, then consider carefully what "fitness" means to you, because different styles of martial arts exercise the body in different ways. Vigorous forms—with a lot of kicking and jumping—offer cardiovascular fitness and stress release, while the more quiet forms tone muscles and regulate body functions. Schools offering long sessions with vigorous activity will suit the person who is mainly out for exercise.

Five Common Reasons People Study Kung fu:

1. Combat sport

2. Self-defense

3. Physical fitness

4. Performance

5. Cultural interest

A fourth reason is performance. Some people just like the look of it (or, more accurately, like the look of what they've perhaps seen in "kung fu movies"). Modern wushu is largely for competition and performance, so the forms being created and taught by wushu/kung fu schools are designed to display grace, speed, and agility with dramatic acrobatic movements. As with gymnastics, people may study at these sorts of schools because they want to develop those qualities and/or to perform in tournaments and public displays.

Other people study kung fu for cultural reasons. They have interest in the traditional arts of China or in its philosophies and want to deepen their understanding through physical participation. (Even Confucius encouraged his followers to study both the literary and martial arts.) The martial arts have long been known to build strong character as well as strong bodies. Traditional schools and instructors will probably better suit students with these interests in mind.

Style of Kung fu

One aspect in the choice of school is the type of kung fu being taught. While there are many styles of kung fu in the world, there are only a handful being taught widely in the U.S., and the number being taught in your area could be very small. Fortunately, at the beginning stages the style of kung fu is not as important as the instructor and the quality of the school. Many of the techniques (stances, punches, kicks, and so on) are very similar in all styles. Once you have a firm foundation in any one style, you should easily be able to pick up another or others. Thus, you may start in a style that doesn't quite attract you because you've found a good sifu or school nearby and feel confident that your time and effort will not be wasted. Indeed, this could be to your advantage, because, when you do have the chance to study the style of your choice, you will be able to make rapid progress from a well-laid foundation.

If you have a choice of styles, consider your natural build. Tall, long-limbed people are better suited for northern styles, while shorter people tend to be better suited for southern styles.

On the other hand, if it so happens that you do have a choice of styles, then by all means consider this factor in your choice. Chapter 3 includes descriptions of the most popular forms of kung fu currently being taught in the U.S.; you can undoubtedly get more information from the school itself—both from talking to the instructors and from watching the students at work.

Style of School

A third factor to consider is the style of school. Kung fu is an ancient art, handed down through generations, over centuries, and now across cultures, and thus, the style of its teaching has naturally evolved. In the past, political and social pressures influenced the status of the martial arts; today, economic conditions and cultural norms create new pressures, influencing how and to whom the art is taught. In China in the past, kung fu skills were traditionally taught individually, handed down from a master to selected students. Money was not an issue; often a good student paid no fees and was possibly supported by the master. In contrast, in the West today, public class teaching has become the norm, and kung fu tends to be taught more like other Western athletic disciplines and sports, in large schools supported by the tuition of students. The result is a range in school styles from traditional/Chinese to modern/Western, and any specific school will fall somewhere between the ends of that spectrum. A new student out to choose a school should be aware of this range in school styles and then choose what he or she finds most comfortable.

Traditional Schools

In the old days, a kung fu school was structured and run much like a family. There was mutual commitment between student and teacher in the context of shared historical and cultural traditions. The teacher accepted the student like a son or daughter with the responsibility to teach, guide, and support students in their studies and development. Likewise, the student accepted the teacher like a parent with the responsibility to respect and obey him or her, and to study with full devotion to the art and dedication to the school. And both teacher and student felt appreciation of and responsibility to the long line of teachers and students that went before them, because it was only these previous efforts that had preserved the art and made the present learning possible.

Traditional and modern schools differ in teaching style and in what is expected of students.

This means that, in a traditional school, there is a strong presence of Chinese cultural traditions. There is a hierarchy of respect and responsibility among students, and there are subtle obligations above and beyond the mere learning and teaching of fighting strategies and techniques. In these schools, learning kung fu is part of the greater education of mind and character. Older (that is, more advanced) students will often spend time with the teacher(s) after class; they will assume duties around the school (for example, cleaning); and social events will be organized for holidays and special occasions. They will also assume responsibilities for teaching the younger or newer students.

The teaching style in a strongly traditional school also differs. The teacher, or sifu, will often teach more individually, according to each student's capabilities and much more in the context of long-term development than short-term gains. The teacher-student relationship tends to grow in depth and breadth over time. That is, in the beginning the sifu may be assessing the student's commitment, discipline, and inner qualities, even more than his or her physical abilities. As the student shows sincerity, so the sifu will extend the teaching, matching the commitment of the student. Thus, learning in a traditional-style school could require much more self-discipline and be much more personally challenging.

How Much Does It Cost?

*G*enerally, the cost of kung fu study will consist of tuition to the school plus the cost of clothes. Some schools ask that you wear their uniform—which they will usually sell at the school. No equipment is usually needed at the beginning stages. Testing and tournament fees vary widely and are, to a certain extent, optional.

Modern Schools

In contrast, a kung fu school leaning toward the modern end of the spectrum will be structured much more like classes in other Western athletic sports or disciplines. The responsibilities between teacher and student are much more limited in scope. Generally, classes are large; students line up for workouts and follow the instructor as he or she goes through the routines. Then, typically, students break up into smaller groups to work on special forms, or according to different levels of ability, for special instruction. Time in class is usually well structured. This sort of school is very suitable for people who have limited time and energy to commit to their workouts, who simply want to get some exercise and training, and who like the structure (and greater anonymity) of the group sessions.

Assessing Schools

Once you know your motives and understand the spectrum of school styles—from traditional to modern—the next step is to see what is available in your area. To find schools, you may ask your friends for recommendations or look for advertisements in the phone book, on the Internet, in recreation centers, and so on.

Then visit schools that seem promising. The best approach is to call in advance, find out when you might come watch a class, and then make an appointment. When visiting, you should be assessing the school itself, the teacher, and the students, as well as what is being taught. All will give you clues as to whether this is the place for you.

First, assess the school itself. Is it clean, spacious, well equipped? You may see modern weight-training equipment as well as racks of weapons and trophies. Wall mirrors are very useful for correcting movements and learning new postures. If it is a traditional school, some area of the practice room will likely be set aside to commemorate past masters and/or to show devotion to the art. In the old days, there would have been an altar with incense, fruit, and a statue

Factors to Consider in Evaluating Schools

Facilities	Classes
Students	Teacher

or painting of Guan Gong, legendary general and patron saint of justice and the martial arts; today, one may find photographs of past grand masters and calligraphy. These are meant to inspire students and remind them of their responsibilities, their goals, and the cultural heritage of kung fu; they are not religious symbols.

As for the teacher, find out his or her background. Whom did he learn from? How long has she been studying? How many styles does he know/teach? Do you think she is qualified? Do you like his forms, her style? Does he personally instruct, or do senior students do most of the teaching? Can she explain theory as well as applications of the techniques being taught? Assessing the teacher is admittedly difficult, especially for a beginner. Not all teachers from China are necessarily good; not all Westerners are necessarily second-rate. Knowing more than one style is almost necessary to truly understand the techniques, but no one can be a "master" of any style (much less more than one style) unless one devotes one's life exclusively to practice. The more a person studies kung fu, the more humble he or she should become—as well as more skillful. The longer people teach, the better they should be. But, even so, all great teachers start somewhere as beginners too. Follow your "gut instincts." Rather than analyzing a teacher's background too critically, perhaps simply try to determine whether you could get along with this teacher and whether you feel you could learn effectively from him or her.

Watch a class. First, see if the teaching style suits you. In some schools, classes are quite formal, and students practice together in ranks. In other schools, students learn and practice individually with the teacher circulating among the students correcting them as necessary. Some people prefer the discipline of a class; others enjoy the freedom of self-study. Second, see if you like the look of what students are learning. Does this style of kung fu appeal to you? Is this what you would like to do yourself? If some of the students are doing spectacular aerial acrobatics that you think are totally beyond your abilities, do not be put off. First, such techniques are not essential—they are not fundamental aspects of kung fu, nor are they necessary to learn. Second, you really don't know what you can do until you train, have instruction, and then try!

Next, after class is over talk to students. How long have they been studying? How often do they come to class? Are they dedicated? If they've been studying a long time at the same school and come regularly, then it is likely that they are satisfied both with the quality of the teaching and their progress.

Do you like the students? Are they the kind of people you would like to become? Kung fu is more than mere physical exercise; it is also a journey in self-development. If you like how these students are developing, then this is likely to be a path you too will benefit from. Furthermore, once you join, the older students will become your teachers, so you should be prepared to give them respect.

Finally, you must consider cost in terms of both time and money. Can you afford it now? In the long run? Is the school convenient to your home or work? Will you be able to arrive at class on time, regularly? These are practical questions that need to be considered as well.

The Single Most Important Factor

Certainly, many factors should be considered in choosing a kung fu school, and we have tried to describe the more important ones above. But if you talk to seasoned students, they will emphatically and unflinchingly insist that the single most critical factor in choosing a kung fu school is, and should be, the teacher (or the sifu, as a teacher is traditionally called in Cantonese). Do you like him? Does he accept you as his student? If the answer is yes, then everything else will fall into place. If you like the sifu, like his style, appreciate his teaching—then you will come to class, you will learn, you will progress, and you will find the commitment to weather the inevitable periods of discouragement and disappointment. If you like the sifu, then you will probably like the style of the school, you will probably like the other students who are studying there—and they will probably like you.

This traditional phrase describes what qualities a student should look for in seeking a teacher: "Martial ethics/virtue comes first"—not fighting prowess.

Studying kung fu should be a lifelong commitment to personal development of body and mind. The techniques come from a particular cultural tradition, but the qualities and the virtues inherent in the study are universal. In choosing your school, go for the one that can help you be your best.

Do You Need a School At All?

A final question that may have occurred to you, as you contemplate studying kung fu, is whether you need a school at all. Couldn't you just learn from this, or some other, book together with videos? These resources are widely available, especially from martial arts supply stores and Web sites. The short answer is that you may not need a school, but you definitely need a teacher.

The long answer is more complex and partly dependent on your nature. At the beginning levels, you may be able to learn the basic stances from pictures and descriptions. You can begin to train muscles, open joints, and stretch. This mostly requires time and effort. As you advance, however, your needs will become more complex, just as the moves themselves become more complex. You will need demonstrations, personal guidance, and feedback on what you are doing. There is a rhythm to learning the forms; there are subtleties of technique that you must see in action in person and that you probably will not see until you are trained. Furthermore, there is great value in group work; you can learn much from fellow students, including the feeling of combat in sparring.

If you live in an area where there really are no schools, or if it is just not financially possible for you to enroll in a school, but you are determined to study, then by all means begin. Use this book, and any others you can find, to begin training and developing muscle, coordination, balance, and flexibility. Meanwhile, look for your chance to find a teacher or to attend a seminar—to somehow learn in person.

Finding a Good Student

Kung fu is a living art that can only be transmitted from person to person. This is partly why the personal relationship between teacher and student is so critical. It also means that, just as you are looking for a good teacher, so every teacher is looking for a good student. And for the teacher, finding a good student is absolutely essential for the survival of the art. So if you are a good student, with sincere respect and dedication, then you will be welcome in any kung fu school, regardless of your physical ability.

According to this traditional phrase, "Finding a teacher is difficult; finding a student is even harder."

求師難，求徒更難。

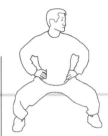

chapter 5
what to wear

THE CLOTHES AND EQUIPMENT you will need very much depend on the school. Some schools like their students to wear a common uniform, and, in such cases, the school will usually sell what is required. Other schools allow students to dress as they like, although they often have guidelines. The following gives a general idea of what to expect.

Figure 5-1: A traditional kung fu uniform, including a jacket, loose pants, sash, and shoes—all in black

Respect

The first principle to remember is that what you wear expresses your attitude and should show respect to the sifu, the school, and the art. Specifically this means:

1. Make sure whatever you wear is clean and neat, without holes, and is appropriate for a serious workout.
2. Do not wear a uniform from another martial art (such as karate).
3. Do not wear a uniform with a logo or emblem from another kung fu school.

Let your kung fu uniform be a symbol and reminder of your commitment to your teacher, to your school, and to the generations of teachers before you whose dedication preserved the art and made your training possible.

The Basic Uniform

Colors

The traditional color for kung fu clothes is black—shirts, sashes, pants, and shoes. There are exceptions. In some schools, instructors may wear white to distinguish themselves from the students and make it easy for students to spot them to ask them questions. In sparring opponents may wear different-colored shirts. Schools of some styles are adopting different colored sashes to indicate rank, as in karate. For demonstrations colorful uniforms (especially in silk) are appropriate, especially for wushu, but black is generally the standard color for kung fu clothes and footwear.

> *Shoes are critical. Choose a pair that allows ankle flexibility for kicks and low stances and has adequate cushioning for workouts on hard floors.*

Shoes

You must wear shoes; kung fu is not done in bare feet. (This is consistent with its origins as a form of self-defense in daily life.) Shoes should be sturdy, lightweight, and flexible. They must allow free ankle movement, which is required for toe and heel kicks and some of the deep stances. The soles should provide cushioning for stomping, should provide some traction—that is, they should not be slippery—but should not have deep treads that could interfere with executing smooth floor sweeps. They should not have metal buckles that might cause injury in kicking. Many people find that skateboard shoes are ideal. Beware of shoes made in China. While they appear more traditional and can be cheap, they may not be very functional. They have no arch, and some have thin, hard rubber soles that can be quite uncomfortable, if not painful. (If you like the style, wearing heavy socks may provide enough cushioning for comfort.)

Pants

Traditional kung fu pants are made of cotton. They typically have elastic cuffs at the bottoms of the legs and elastic as well as a drawstring at the waist. They are cut loose, if not baggy, often with an extra triangular piece of fabric sewn into the crotch to ensure freedom of movement for high kicks and jumps. When wearing a sash, students may wear one-size-larger pants so that the elastic band can be positioned above the sash, while the legs will still be long enough to "blouse" slightly at the ankles.

Sashes

Sashes are generally not worn by beginners; however, they may be commonly worn by senior students and instructors. Sashes are typically made of silk, six to nine inches wide and nine to fourteen feet long. The proper length of the sash is determined by the person's waist: twice the waist measurement is the minimum, while four times the waist measurement is considered more desirable and more comfortable. Black is the traditional color, but other colors are being adopted by some schools as an indication of rank, much like the karate system.

> The sash helps support the lower back and control the breathing center.

Originally, the sash worn in China served other purposes, in addition to simply holding up the pants. First, it was worn to support the lower back and control the breathing center (the *dan tian*). Second, very practically, it was used to conceal small weapons. The sash also served as a symbol of one's country and ancestors, and the way it was tied indicated rank. Masters of literature and calligraphy wore their sashes tied on the left; masters of martial arts, in the middle; while martial arts students wore theirs tied on the right.

The proper way to tie the sash is a traditional technique that the instructor will demonstrate when needed.

Shirts/Jackets

In most schools cotton T-shirts are worn in the summer and sweatshirts in the winter. In some schools—especially large schools—the instructors and assistant instructors (senior students) may wear white shirts. This makes them conspicuous, so beginning students can easily distinguish instructors from students to ask them questions. Also, sometimes for two-person forms, one participant will wear a white shirt and the other a black shirt to distinguish the two sides of the form.

Extra Equipment

For Protection

For free-sparring protective equipment such as headgear, gloves, groin protection, and mouth protection should be worn by both men and women. Beginners will not need this equipment because free sparring usually begins only at the intermediate level after students have learned two-person forms and prearranged sparring.

For Competitions and Performances

For competitions, tournaments, and public performances, the school may ask students who will be participating to dress uniformly (for example, T-shirt with the school logo and black pants or a special costume). For these occasions participants will usually be told well in advance what they need to buy and how/where to buy it.

chapter 6
etiquette

PARTICULARLY in traditional kung fu schools, students are expected to observe certain rules of conduct. Some of the rules are simple courtesy; others derive from tradition, and still others may be unique to your school. Almost all are based on principles of respect: respect for the art, for masters both past and present, for fellow students, and for one's self. They help instill in every student the qualities and virtues that define the character of the true martial artist.

Whatever the rules of the school, all students should try to follow them as closely as possible. At the same time, do not be terrified of breaking a rule, as if you are committing a crime. If, or when, as a beginner, you forget, an older student will probably quietly remind you of proper behavior. Make the correction, and carry on. Of course, if any student continuously breaks a rule or refuses to follow a school's regulations, he or she will probably be asked to leave.

A typical set of rules and etiquette for a kung fu school might include the following.

Bowing/Saluting

When entering and leaving the school, bowing—or using the kung fu salute—is appropriate. Saluting the Chief Instructor (sifu) is also appropriate, as is giving the salute to the assistant instructor teaching your specific class. Upon entering and leaving, it may also be customary to salute other students.

New students will probably be taught the proper salute during the orientation session or the first class. Each style has its own particular salute. One of the most traditional involves placing the right fist in the palm of the left hand, holding the two hands in front of the chest, and inclining the head and upper body slightly in the direction of the person being saluted. This salute comes from the days of the Ching dynasty, when Ming dynasty supporters used this

"sun,"   "moon,"

"brightness"

salute to identify each other. The flat left hand represented the Chinese symbol for "moon," while the fist represented the symbol for "sun"; together, these two symbols compose the character *"ming,"* meaning brightness. It is also said that this salute symbolizes a weapon (right fist) that is in its scabbard (left palm), meaning that there will be no fighting.

Personal Appearance and Hygiene

Dress

While in the school, always dress appropriately. In most cases this will mean wearing your kung fu uniform. It should be clean. Do not wear a hat or sunglasses. Do not wear jewelry of any sort (rings, earrings, body piercings, watches, and so on) as these can interfere with your movements and even cause injury to yourself or another person during training.

Personal Hygiene

As you will be working closely with other students and exerting yourself strenuously, come to school clean. As you may be exchanging punches and kicks, especially later in your training, it's best to get in the habit of keeping your fingernails neatly trimmed.

Behavior in Class

Arrive on time to show respect for your teacher and fellow students.

Show a positive attitude and try your best in every assignment. Naturally, you will like some forms and some movements better than others; naturally, you will be better at some than at others. In spite of these preferences, give each movement your best effort. Striving to maintain this attitude is also part of the training.

During group training, ask questions only when given the opportunity; do not interrupt teaching. If you are unclear about anything, wait until after the group session to clarify your misunderstanding with an instructor—not with a fellow student. In that way you can be sure you will learn correctly and not disturb others.

Do not chew gum. Often schools will also ask you not to eat in the school except on special occasions.

As for mobile/cell phones, find out what the school's policy on this is, and follow the rule. Some sifus don't like phone calls interfering with class and distracting all the students. (Indeed, some sifus don't even answer their own phone during class time.)

Do not handle or experiment with any of the equipment in the school until you are invited to use it and/or instructed in how to use it. Most schools have various kinds of equipment to help develop muscles and coordination— such as punching bags, wooden dummies, and other floor equipment. You will be shown how to use these things in due time.

Similarly, do not touch or handle any of the weapons that may be on display in the school. In many schools an abundance of weapons of different sizes and shapes—staffs, swords, sabers, chains, and so forth—may be hung on the walls or set in racks around the edges of the practice area. Some of these weapons may belong to individuals, who store them at the school for their use during practice sessions; others belong to the school. In any case, they are not yours, and they are not toys; the best approach is to admire them but not to touch them.

> ## When Can I Start to Use Weapons?
>
> Generally, students do not begin learning weapons until after at least one year practicing hand forms. This varies depending on school policy, the sifu, and the student.

Relations with Others

Other Students

Show respect to all fellow students, regardless of their rank or ability.

Do not correct or criticize other people, either to their faces or behind their backs. If you see someone else doing something that you think is wrong, do not correct him or her. Instead, you should probably ask an instructor to make sure *you* are not doing something wrong.

Do not compare yourself with other students, or your progress with theirs. Do not think poorly of those who seem to be less capable than you. Similarly, do not show off. Neither of these attitudes will help you improve. No matter how well or poorly you are doing, there is always someone who is doing better than you—and also someone doing worse. Focus on your own practice and form.

Do not give in to ego, anger, or aggression for any reason, either in the school or on the street. Kung fu is a discipline of self-defense, self-control, and self-development. Do not use it for intimidation, revenge, bullying, or coercion.

Do not chat or talk to others during instruction; practice should be pursued earnestly. As you become friendly with your fellow students, there will be a great temptation to socialize during sessions. Don't do it! Save conversation for after class.

Attitude toward the Sifu

Always show respect to the Chief Instructor or master. In a traditional school you will always address your teacher as sifu (Cantonese dialect) or *shifu* (Beijing/Mandarin dialect), the Chinese name for "teacher." Whenever the sifu gives instruction, thank him or her—and you may bow and/or give the salute in appreciation. In some schools the sifu's office is considered special; students may not enter without permission, and inside the office there may be specific seats designated for higher-ranked students or assistant instructors. (The newcomer should simply follow the lead of older students or ask permission.)

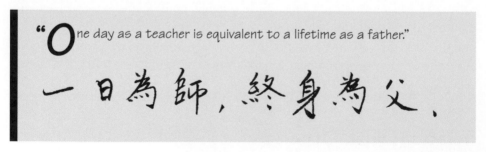

"*O*ne day as a teacher is equivalent to a lifetime as a father."

一 日 為 師, 終 身 為 父.

It is also considered impolite, in some schools, to ask the sifu to teach you something in particular. Out of respect for the sifu's experience in teaching and understanding of your needs and level, you should wait for him or her to decide what you should learn and when you are ready to progress to another form. This is particularly true for beginners.

Relations with Visitors

In some, more open schools, visitors may enter the school and begin to ask questions of the first student they see—which could be you. Such questions from visitors and callers should always be referred to a senior student or the sifu.

Behavior outside the School

Once you join a school, you become a representative of that school. Your behavior both inside and outside the school should reflect positively on both the school and the tradition of martial arts. Never criticize other martial artists, whether of your school, of another school, or of another branch of martial arts.

You should not teach outsiders, including your friends, what you are learning in the school—until or unless you are designated an instructor. To teach when you are not qualified is not only disrespectful but also dangerous. Kung fu is a subtle art and teaching is a serious responsibility; until you are well versed in the art, you may not realize what you don't know, and thus, you may not teach correctly, which could do more damage than good to your unsuspecting friend.

師 The word "si" means teacher or master, as does the longer form "sifu." In the forms of address given here, "si" refers to one and the same teacher. That is, only those students who learned under the same master would refer to each other using the "si-" forms of address (si hing, si je, and so on).

Forms of Address

At traditional schools you may sometimes hear the traditional Chinese forms of address rather than personal names. This may be confusing for the new student, but familiarity grows with time; don't feel embarrassed in the meantime. Using these forms emphasizes the relationships within the school as a "family" and generally strengthens the school spirit; they are not used for pretension or intimidation. (Note that the following names are given in the Cantonese dialect of the Chinese language, as this is the most common among kung fu schools.)

Master of the school, or Chief Instructor (male or female): sifu
Fellow students:
   In southern-style schools names are assigned according to age:
      Students who are older than you: *si hing* (male), *si je* (female)
      Students who are the same age as you or younger than you: *si daih* (male), *si muih* (female)
   In northern-style schools names are assigned according to how long you have learned from a particular sifu:
      Students who have studied longer than you: si hing (male), si je (female)
      Students who have studied for a shorter time than you: si daih (male), si muih (female)
   For students who have studied more or less the same length of time as you, go by age; address those who are older as si hing/je, those who are younger as si daih/muih.
There are other forms of address—for example, for fellow students of your sifu, for his or her sifu, and the like—but the beginning student will generally not need to be familiar with or use these.

chapter 7
your first class

The Orientation Session

IN SOME SCHOOLS your first class will be an orientation session. At this time you will learn what you need to know to get started, and you will begin to become familiar with how the school operates. Take this opportunity to get to know the people, the location, and the studio, and to ask any questions you might have about any aspect of your beginning training. Don't be shy; the sooner you feel comfortable and confident in the school, the sooner and more quickly you will learn and progress.

Topics that are likely to be covered in the orientation session include the following.

First, you will be told what to wear. The beginner will usually need only shirt, pants, and shoes. These could be generic (for example, black T-shirt, pants, and shoes), or there could be a specific outfit (a T-shirt with the school logo, or the like). The school may have a supply of the clothes required available for sale. If not, then they will be able to tell you where to buy them.

Second, you may be given a list of rules or code of etiquette explaining how to behave while you are in the school. Read this carefully, be aware of what is expected, and try to remember it. The overall guiding principle is courtesy and

When you don't know what to do, follow the lead of older students.

respect for all people at all times. For specifics, watch and follow the lead of older students. This will help you learn the ways of the school without undue embarrassment or awkwardness.

If there is no formal orientation session, then be sure to ask what you need to know about clothing and etiquette before your first class.

When attending class, you will be expected to be punctual, arriving for class on time and staying for the full class period. If for any reason you must arrive late, there may be particular etiquette for how to join a class after it has started. For example, in some schools a tardy student is expected, first, to salute the class/sifu/photo of grandmaster and then to wait on the side until given permission by the instructor to join the class. It may not be appropriate to simply rush in. If this information is not included in the initial orientation lecture, then be sure to ask.

Learn the proper way to join a class when you are late.

During the orientation period, you will probably also be taught any rituals or special forms of salute that you will be expected to use at the school. These are important and should be performed with as much attention and care as any exercise or form.

Finally, during the orientation session, you should have the chance to ask any lingering questions that you may have on any topic related to the school or your training. One of these questions might be how to ask questions during class. It may not be appropriate to interrupt the class or the sifu every

Save questions for the appropriate time.

time you have a question, particularly in a large class with a demonstration. This disturbs other students and interrupts the teacher's train of thought and lesson plan. Generally, it is preferred that you save your questions until the instructor asks for them; meanwhile, continue to pay attention to the demonstration and lecture, because your question may be answered in the course of the teaching. If not, then when you have the chance to ask, do so. Be honest and forthright, both in the orientation session and throughout your training. By sharing your concerns and questions, you open the door for advice and correction. Answers should clear the air, like dispelling fog. The more certain, clear, and confident you are, the more thorough and accurate will be your training.

The First Training Session

After the orientation session will come your first class of training and instruction. Be sure to wear your new uniform and arrive on time. Bring water, but no food.

The form of the class will depend on the school. Having visited the school previously, you should already have some idea of what to expect. In smaller and/or traditional schools, you may be working mainly on your own with short periods of instruction followed by long periods of practice. In larger and/or modern schools, the class may be strictly organized with a definite pattern of activities and with students lined up in ranks. Often after group warm-ups

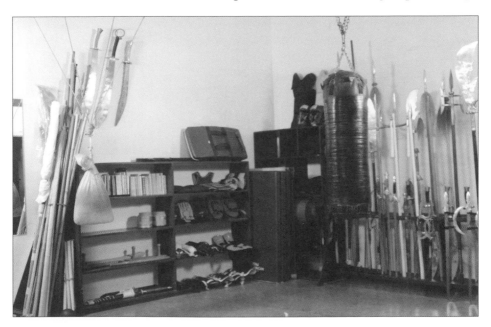

Figure 7-1: The walls of a typical kung fu school, lined with weapons racks, weight-training equipment, mirrors, shelves of reference books, as well as cubbyholes for students' personal belongings

Concentrate on follow-ing instructions. Worrying about how well you are doing will only make you do worse!

there will be a demonstration for all, and then the class will break up into smaller groups for individual practice and instruction. (See chapter 13: "Participating in a Workout," for further details.)

No matter how the school is structured, in class the main point is your attitude. Show respect, listen attentively, and follow instructions to the best of your ability. Work diligently until the end of class. This shows that you are sincerely interested in what you are learning and that you appreciate the instructors' patience and dedication in teaching you. That is really what the instructors are looking for, because, with that kind of attitude, you will be a credit to the school and to the art—and, with such an attitude, progress and achievement are assured. Do not worry about whether you are fast or slow, good or bad. Just concentrate on doing the best you can. You are there to learn, and the instructors are there to help you. Working together with respect and dedication brings success for everyone.

elements

THE MOVEMENTS of kung fu fall roughly into four categories: stances, footwork, kicks, and hand techniques (where "hand" refers to the entire arm). Because all styles of kung fu derive from a common root, these basic elements are very similar. Certainly, individual styles differ in the finer points—some have special, characteristic punches or kicks, for example—but virtually all styles share the fundamentals, and all beginners start by learning them.

Thus, the following pages attempt to present only what is common and fundamental to all styles. The descriptions explain how to execute the various movements, including common pitfalls. Nevertheless, certain styles (or certain sifus) may differ in the details of how the basic punches, kicks, or blocks are executed; in such cases, students should follow their own teachers.

chapter 8
stances

I**N KUNG FU** standing positions, or "stances," are the first basic elements that a beginner will be taught. And the beginner should practice them diligently because stances are the physical foundation from which all technique is launched. Martial artists at every level of skill in virtually every style of kung fu continue to practice stances throughout their training.

Practicing Stances

Why Practice Stances?

Practicing stances builds strong muscles, improves balance, increases endurance, and develops a stable center of gravity in a variety of positions. This stability is essential to good technique.

Practicing stances helps develop a stable center of gravity, which is essential to all techniques.

Furthermore, mastering the stances trains the body to automatically assume correct and stable positions as it moves from position to position in the course of a form (or fight). Footwork is, essentially, moving from stance to stance. Thus, with well-developed stances, you will feel confident in assuming any position you need to as you dodge or deliver an attack. A traditional kung fu saying is that power originates in the foot, is activated by the leg, and is guided in application by the waist. In this sense, stances—the feet—are the literal foundation of martial arts technique.

The more you practice, the more you will experience and appreciate the value of a good, strong stance.

How to Practice

In practicing stances always spend equal time doing right and left versions, and vary them during practice to rest the muscles. Check your positions constantly to make sure your feet and legs are in the right orientation and alignment, especially in relation to each other. Also check to make sure your back and shoulders are relaxed but straight and your upper body is centered over your lower body. Get to know how each stance feels; practice until you become thoroughly grounded and comfortable in all the stances.

The Basic Eight Stances

Horse stance

Forward stance

Cat stance

Heel stance

X-stance

Crane stance

Back stance

Kneeling stance

The Basic Eight

The following eight stances are considered basic and are a part of virtually every kung fu style. Each style may, in addition, have other stances, which the beginner will be introduced to in due time, but they are mostly variations of these elementary eight.

You will note that arm position is not mentioned in the descriptions below. Arm position varies with the particular application, or use, of the stance, so strictly speaking, it is not part of the stance. For practice you may simply hold your arms at your sides, elbows bent, hands clenched in fists resting at your waist.

Horse Stance

The horse stance is the foundation stance of all styles of kung fu, if not of most styles of Asian martial arts. Students are asked to train in this stance for long periods of time, beginning with a few minutes and building up to (in the "olden days") hours. It is legendary that a master, seeking to test the determination, dedication, and discipline of a new student, would ask him or her to train in the horse stance for hours a day over a period of weeks or months before begin-

Figure 8-1: Horse stance

ning to teach the student anything else.

Why is the horse stance so valuable? First and most obviously, it trains the body. Assuming this stance for long periods of time requires strong thigh muscles, and the lower you go, the more vigorous the training. The thigh muscles are the largest in the body and are responsible for kicks, jumps, and virtually all movement of the entire body. Thus, the stronger they are, the better your footwork and the greater your endurance will be. This stance will also strengthen the knees and gradually, with concentration, open the hip joints. Open hip joints will free the legs for a wider range of movement, the delivery of greater power in kicks, and greater speed in footwork. All of the above, together, give stability: Once in the stance, you will develop a strong sense of being firmly rooted to the ground. This sense is essential for maintaining balance as you execute hand and foot techniques, both in forms and in actual fighting situations.

According to Chinese medical theory, the horse stance helps generate courage.

Second, and perhaps less obviously, the horse stance trains the mind. Simply being able to remain in the stance for long periods requires discipline. Once settled in a stance, the stability brings calmness. For any martial artist— indeed, for anyone under pressure to act, from soldiers to athletic contestants to victims in emergencies—the first rule is: Stay calm. If you panic, you will forget everything, and no matter how much training you have done, it will be of no use. According to Chinese medical theory, standing in the horse stance reinforces the energy of certain body meridians and thereby generates courage. This is the only stance that produces this fundamental quality, without which all training, all strength, and all strategy are lost. From Shaolin Temple days, this has been known, and the horse stance has, thus, been practiced since the earliest days of Asian martial arts and is still highly revered today.

Assuming the Stance

Place your feet parallel, wider than shoulders' width (see Figure 8-1). Lower your body ("sink into the position"). Open the hips, allowing your knees to extend out over your feet (but not beyond). Keep your back straight, shoulders relaxed, head erect and balanced on top of your spine. Your weight should be evenly distributed between both feet.

The upper body can be in any of a variety of positions, depending on the training effect desired. For standing meditation the arms may be held in front of the body making a broad circle, as though holding a large ball, and the palms either facing the body or pointed outward with fingertips approximately pointed at each other. For development of arm strength, you may hold your arms outstretched to the side, level with your shoulders (be sure to relax your shoulders), fingers also outstretched. For a fighting position arms may be bent, and elbows back with hands clenched as fists, held at the waist; this version expands the chest.

The degree of workout is determined by how low you go and by how long you hold the stance. The lower you go, the more vigorous the workout, but never let your hips sink below your knees; that is, the thighs should always be inclined at least slightly toward the knees. Start with a few minutes, ideally each day, and gradually increase to twenty, thirty, or as many minutes as you can spend. The effort will bring many benefits.

Training Tips

Keep your back straight and perpendicular to the ground with one line through the head, down the spine, through the tailbone, and into the ground. If there is a mirror nearby, check your posture. There are two common mistakes: one is hunching the shoulders and leaning the whole torso forward; the other is creating a swayback posture in which the small of the back is curved in and the stomach is pushed out. To correct the first problem, make sure your shoulders are back and your head sits freely on top of your spine, merely balanced there without need of muscular support. As for the second mistake, this is typically a problem of the pelvis. Keep the tailbone tucked down by tilting the

Avoid these common mistakes in doing the horse stance:

☞ Hunching forward

☞ Arching the back

top of the pelvis backward, thus flattening the small of the back. This will lengthen the spine and give you the sense of being taller. There should be no inward curve at the base of the spine in the kidney region. This is critical for three reasons: First, if you hold a swayback for a long time, you can develop lower-back pain, as this posture tends to squeeze the kidneys; second, for advanced training, such a position will interfere with the flow of qi (vital energy); third, such a position will limit the strength you can develop in the rest of your back for supporting punching and kicking.

Your knees should be directed outward, thus spreading the hip joint and focusing weight over the feet. Use your mind to relax the muscles at your hip and gradually open the joints.

Your toes should be either parallel or pointed *slightly* outward (not more than 20 degrees). If they are pointed strongly outward, balance is compromised and you will easily fall over. (You may check this yourself by assuming the position and asking someone to try to push you over.) Your toes should grip the ground. Weight distribution on each foot should be 60 percent on the front (ball) of the foot and 40 percent on the heel of the foot; that is, more toward the front than the back, as it is the toes of the foot that will initiate movement. Pay attention not only to front-back distribution but also to inside-outside distribution: ideally, the weight should be concentrated on the outside edges of the feet. This creates a very stable stance, activates the muscles on the outsides of the lower part of the legs, and reduces the strain on the knees.

Forward, Front, or Bow Stance (Left, Right)

Like the horse stance, the forward stance is an elementary and fundamental position. For the beginner it introduces uneven weight distribution and the use of that distribution to support technique. The main value of the front stance is to enable delivery of full power through the front. In application the stance may not be held for long, but in training hold it longer in order to strengthen the thigh of your forward leg and stretch the hamstring of your back leg.

Assuming the Stance

From the horse stance, pivot on the balls of your feet, in either direction: For a right forward stance, turn your torso to the right and turn your feet so that

both point 45 degrees to the left (or turn the back foot a few degrees less). Bend your right leg until the knee is over the toes—but not beyond. Shift a little more than half your body's weight onto the right (forward) leg, maintaining balance and solidity with a push forward from your left (rear) thigh. Weight distribution should be 60/40: 60 percent on the forward leg, 40 percent on the rear leg. Keep your upper body relaxed, erect, and facing directly forward, centered over your feet.

A left front stance is a mirror image of the right; that is, lean forward on your left foot/leg, pushing with the back/right leg to support the stance.

Figure 8-2: Left forward stance

The forward stance enables delivery of full power through the front.

Training Tips

Far and away the most common mistake is that the back foot is pointed too far to the side. It should be pointed either 30 or 45 degrees out from the front centerline or straight ahead. When it is pointed more than 45 degrees out to the side, balance is weak and damage to the knee can easily occur. Be careful! A second common error is in the relative alignment of front and back feet. They should not be directly in front of each other. Instead, the toes of the front foot should be in line with the heel of the back foot, so that a forward punch will come out between the feet. That is, if parallel lines were drawn forward from the heels of the two feet, the line of the punch would come out between those two parallel lines. This position will keep your body stable.

For a strong, stable forward stance, the orientation of the two feet is critical.

Cat or Tiger Stance (Left, Right)

The cat stance is primarily a retreating stance used to reposition the body in preparation for a kick. Of course, it can be used for other purposes (for example, for a knee strike), but in most applications the cat stance positions the leg for a quick kick.

Figure 8-3: Cat stance

Assuming the Stance

From the forward stance, shift your weight onto the back leg; bring the front leg back with knee bent and toe tip touching the ground. The bent knee should point straight forward, and the toes should touch the ground in line with the heel of the back foot— either just in front of the back foot or a bit farther (distance is personal; an intermediate position is most stable).

In some styles only the tip of the toe touches the ground; in others all the toes and the ball of the foot touch the ground. In the former case, all the weight is on the back leg, and the toe tip merely steadies the body. In the latter case, 5–10 percent of the body weight is on the front leg (toes). Keep your upper body erect, relaxed, and alert.

You can move into a cat stance from any stance; here, for descriptive purposes, the forward stance is used because the back foot is then oriented properly (that is, at 45 degrees).

Training Tips

The back foot must be at 45 degrees—not pointing forward parallel to the front toe/foot, and not pointing at 90 degrees, perpendicular to the front foot. Weight should be 90–100 percent on your back foot; in other words, virtually all of your weight is on your back leg, which must be firm and stable. Do not lock your back knee; this leg must retain some spring, which will be essential for the next move—whether it propels your body forward or delivers a kick. For stability your front foot must be slightly to the side—not directly in front—of your back foot.

Heel Stance (Left, Right)

Also known as the "negative" stance or "seven-star stance," the heel stance is a slight variation of the cat stance with very different applications. The heel stance is mainly used to cause an opponent to fall by catching his ankle in a foot lock or by causing her to trip.

Assuming the Stance

Stand as in the cat stance, but the heel—not the toe(s)—of your front foot should touch the ground. Point your toes up and inward, like a hook or latch.

Rest 5–10 percent of your body weight on the front heel. Keep the knee of your back leg slightly bent, never locked. Keep your upper body erect, relaxed, alert, and facing forward.

Training Tips

Common mistakes with this stance are: putting too much weight on the front foot (there should be virtually none—only the heel rests on the ground); positioning the feet one in front of the other (very unstable), rather than slightly apart; not pointing the raised toes inward (for hooking an opponent's foot); and locking the knee of the back leg. Be sure your hips are centered and stable over your feet, not

Figure 8-4: Heel stance

pushed to the side over one leg (particularly over the leg bearing your body weight).

Figure 8-5: X-stance

X-Stance, or Cross Stance (Left, Right)

This stance is used either to retreat or to move forward over a greater distance than is possible with any other move except a jump. Thus, an X-stance shift (see chapter 9, "Footwork") covers as much ground as a jump but is safer than a jump, in one sense, because one foot is always on the ground. Its other special value is that it moves you (forward, backward, or sideways) without changing the orientation of your upper body.

In terms of applications, this is a very versatile and valuable stance. In executing it, you can either move or not move your shoulders: that is, you can use an X-stance to get closer to your opponent, moving your shoulders to extend the reach of a front punch. It can also be used to retreat from an attempt to throw you off balance or to take you down from behind with a leg sweep. In this situation turning with an X-stance can release you from a foot sweep and put you in a position to throw/knock your opponent down.

Note: Because of the unusual arrangement of the knee in this stance, doing it improperly can easily damage the knees. Beginners should train in this stance only under the supervision of an instructor!

Assuming the Stance

Set one foot facing forward. Slide the other leg behind it, setting the toes and ball of the foot down, heel up, with 10 percent of your weight on this back, "Xed" leg. Keep the toes of the unmoved foot pointing forward; this leg should bear most of the body's weight. Your upper body should be erect; it may remain facing to the front, or it may rotate with the leg, depending on the application.

Training Tips

The toes of your front leg should be at a 90-degree angle (perpendicular) to the line of the stance. Your front knee should not be locked and should bear most of your body weight. Your back leg must be extended behind your front leg; that is, your back knee will be behind your front knee, although your back leg could be fully or partially extended, depending on the application/situation. This orientation is for balance.

Figure 8-6: Crane stance

Crane Stance (Left, Right)

Similar to the cat stance, this stance also develops balance but demands more skill due to a higher center of gravity. It is used to prepare for kicks, knee strikes, and hops; it can also be used as a foot block or knee strike.

Assuming the Stance

From the cat stance, raise the bent leg until your toes barely touch the opposite knee. Keep the toes pointed. (Styles differ in the precise orientation of the raised foot—in some styles the toes point to the side; in others they point down, and so forth.) Your back leg should be straight, but not locked (keep the knee slightly bent).

Training Tips

Beginners typically have trouble with this stance because they can't hold their balance. The best way to improve is to start training with a cat stance (that is, with no weight on the front toe) and then gradually learn to lift your knee. To speed progress and develop even greater stability, close your eyes (or use a blindfold) as you practice. The foot of your raised leg should not dangle in the air, nor should it rest on the knee—it should just touch in whatever orientation is appropriate for the style you are learning.

Figure 8-7: Back stance

Back Stance (Left, Right)

This stance resembles the horse stance (or front stance) in the position of the feet, but the weight is distributed differently. This can be used to execute a foot sweep and also to execute a side punch while leaning your body back, out of reach of your opponent.

Assuming the Stance

Stand in a horse stance. Shift your weight to one side, bending one leg and straightening the other. Look to the side, over the straightened leg. When the stance is complete, your back leg should bear 60–70 percent of the weight, and your front leg 30–40 percent.

Training Tips

The toes of your extended (front) leg must be turned inward. Leaving the toes pointed forward puts tremendous pressure on your ankle, tending to pull the joint open; in the long run, you could dislocate your ankle as a result of this pressure.

Kneeling Stance (Left, Right)

This stance has three common uses: (1) When an opponent executes a leg sweep, you can drop into a kneeling stance to lock the sweeping foot, (2) when an opponent makes a high strike to your head, you can dodge it by dropping into a kneeling stance, and (3) you can upset an opponent's balance by dropping into a kneeling stance in which your knee pushes your opponent's knee forward, causing him or her to fall.

Figure 8-8: Kneeling stance

Assuming the Stance

From the front stance, move your back foot halfway toward your front foot, bend your knee, and kneel, lifting the heel of your back foot. Your back knee should come close to the ankle of your front foot. Your front knee should be at the level of your hip or slightly lower; that is, your thigh should be parallel to the ground or slightly angled downward toward the front (so that a ball on your thigh would roll slowly down toward your foot). Your upper body should be erect and facing forward.

Training Tips

Keep your back straight: do not lean forward. This is a challenge, not only for beginners but for more advanced students as well. When your spine is kept erect, you are more alert and able to use the upper part of your body freely; however, this requires strong thigh muscles and good balance. Check the angle of your front thigh. If the knee is too high (that is, if you sink completely into the stance), you will be somewhat "stuck," unable to shuffle forward or backward. The heel of your back foot should rise off the ground with the ball of the foot (not the toes) firmly on the ground. The toes of your front foot should be pointed 45 degrees inward; the entire foot should be flat on the ground.

JUST AS THERE ARE certain basic stances, or standing positions, so there are basic patterns of leg movement, called "footwork," which are used repetitively in any kung fu style. Footwork has two purposes: (1) to upset an opponent's balance and (2) to shift your position. Knowing the purpose, or application, of a specific movement is essential to performing the movement correctly. Thus, the beginner should pay attention to the purpose as well as the execution of any movement.

The Basic Footwork Moves

While moving into or out of any of the basic positions is "footwork," some of the movements are so characteristic that they are given specific names, as described below.

Front Shuffle (Left, Right)

The shuffle allows you to move forward a short distance from a front stance. It is used to bring you closer to your opponent if he or she has stepped or fallen back. To the fighter, the advantage of this technique is that your feet move you closer to the target, but your upper torso remains in the same protective orientation—that is, with one shoulder pointed forward. This is not only safer but also faster than a simple step forward.

Execution

From a front stance, extend your front leg to take a step forward, and drag or slide your back foot to follow, reestablishing a front stance a short distance forward of the original position.

Training Tips

Always move your front foot first, and drag your back foot forward: that is a shuffle. If you first move your back foot forward to meet your front foot, that is an extension (see below). Watch the alignment of your feet. In moving forward you should reestablish a proper front stance just in front of the previous position. Do not move your front foot to the right or left, nor your back foot to the right or left. This could create an unstable position from which you could easily lose balance.

Back Shuffle (Left, Right)

The back shuffle is used to retreat out of range of an opponent's punches or kicks. As with the front shuffle, the body moves in a straight line, maintaining the same orientation of the upper body, which is both safer and faster for establishing a position for the next movement.

Execution

In this case, from a front stance, take a step back with your back foot, and drag your front foot to follow, reestablishing a new front stance somewhat behind the original position.

Training Tips

As in the front shuffle, be sure to move your back foot first, and be careful to maintain the alignment. For some reason maintaining the correct orientation of the feet is more difficult for beginners learning the back shuffle than it is with the forward shuffle, but it is critical. Your two feet should be aligned as if they were on two railroad tracks: parallel and appropriately spaced to give you a solid stance. Without a solid stance you can easily lose balance, and your hand techniques will suffer, losing both accuracy and power.

Simple Forward Extension (Left, Right)

The simple extension moves the body forward farther than the shuffle, but, like the shuffle, it is executed with both feet on the ground. Again, as with shuffles, the upper body remains at an angle toward the opponent, thus reducing exposure and vulnerability.

9-1: Preparing for a simple forward extension

Execution
From a front stance, move your back foot up to your front foot, then immediately step forward with the front foot and reestablish a new front stance.

Training Tips
The distance the back foot moves should be determined by how close or how far away the target is. That is, for a short extension your back foot may move only halfway up to your front foot. For a longer extension it may move beyond the front foot— but, in that case, the back foot always moves in front of the front foot. (If the back foot moves behind the front foot, this is an X-stance shift; see below.) As with shuffles, be careful to reestablish foot alignment in a proper and stable front stance; without a stable stance you compromise the balance, power, and accuracy of subsequent moves (punches, strikes, and so forth).

In addition, watch the orientation of your back foot. When it is placed on the ground, your toes should be in the same (45 degrees outward) orientation as in the original position. This will also help maintain the proper upper-body orientation. If you put your foot down with the toes pointing inward, you will not reestablish a proper front stance, and your shoulders will tend to twist in the direction of the toes. This will defeat the effectiveness of the move.

Retreating Extension (Left, Right)
The extension can also be used to retreat. In this case, from a front stance, your front foot moves back in *front* of your back foot, and then your back foot reestablishes a new front stance. If your front foot moves back behind your back foot, this is an X-stance retreat. As with the forward extension, watch the alignment and orientation of your feet.

Spring Extension (Left, Right), or Hop Forward
The spring extension, as the name suggests, moves the body forward with a

Figure 9-2: Spring extension

spring action, something like a small jump or hop. It is basically a faster and farther version of the simple extension. Of the three forward-moving types of footwork that maintain the front stance and upper-torso orientation, this one propels the body forward the farthest.

Execution

From a front stance, using your front foot as the "springboard," move your back foot beyond your front foot, step down, then immediately step ahead with your front foot, reestablishing a new front stance exactly as at the start.

Training Tips

First, the last foot to land should come down on the heel—not the toes. Just as in walking, the heel hits the ground first. The first foot to land (in the middle of the forward movement) comes down on the toes, but the front foot reestablishes itself with the heel. Second, pay attention to the movement of the knee of the "springboard" foot. The knee should not rise deliberately or noticeably forward; this interferes with the forward thrust of the movement. Instead the knee should naturally fall backward (and out of the way) as it pushes the body forward. Third, check the orientation of your feet after landing. You should finish the extension in a correct and solid front stance. This will keep your shoulders and upper torso in correct position.

Retreating Spring Extension (Left, Right), or Hop Backward

Execution

This movement is executed exactly like the spring extension, but the body moves backward. That is, from a front stance, the front foot moves back, in front of the back foot, while the back leg provides the spring and immediately moves back to reestablish a new front stance well behind the original position.

Figure 9-3: Retreating spring extension

Training Tips

Be sure your front foot moves backward in *front* of the back foot, and be sure to maintain proper orientation and alignment of your two feet after they land. In the hop backward, both feet touch the ground first on the toes, never on the heels.

Cat Stance Shift (Left, Right)

This is fundamentally retreating footwork, to move out of the way of an opponent's attack, while still maintaining a ready position facing him or her. This particular shift puts you in a good position to deliver a kick

Execution

From either left or right cat stance, move in any direction (forward, backward, left, or right), immediately reestablishing a cat stance on the other foot. For example, from a left cat stance, put the raised foot down in a new position, and lift your other foot into a right cat stance.

Training Tips

The main problem with this footwork is not in executing the shift, but in reestablishing a proper cat stance. Remember to keep your upper torso erect, relaxed, but alert, with 90–100 percent of the weight on your back foot and the toes of your front foot only lightly touching the ground.

Crane Stance Shift (Left, Right)

This follows the same principle as the cat stance shift, but it is harder to control and less stable. So it requires stronger balance and better coordination. The crane stance shift or jump can be used to deliver a knee strike or a kick.

Execution

From one crane stance, move in any direction (left, right, forward, or backward), immediately reestablishing a new crane stance on the other leg.

Training Tips

After executing the shift, be sure your new position is stable; that is, you should immediately center and balance your weight on the other leg, with your back erect. From this position you may practice delivering knee strikes and kicks, which will further develop your balance and coordination.

X-Stance Shifts

These four movements are, basically, moving from a front stance into an X-stance. You may go forward, backward, to the side with the front foot, or to the side with the back foot. The unique value of the X-stance shift is that it moves your body to the side while maintaining upper-body (head and torso) position unchanged. In this way you can move around your opponent. Done repetitively from different directions, a series of X-stance shifts can confuse and disorient an opponent.

Execution

In all versions of the X-stance, your upper body must remain erect, facing in the same position as in the original front stance.

X-Stance Retreat

From a front stance, first reorient your back foot slightly outward (90 degrees forward), then slide your front foot back, behind your back foot, so that your legs create an X shape.

X-Stance Advance

From a front stance, move your back foot forward, and position it at a 45- to 90-degree angle. The weight distribution can be anywhere from 20–90 percent on your front foot, depending on the intention, the application, and the orientation of your front foot. The more weight on your front foot, the greater the angle. However, your legs will end up in an X-shaped orientation.

Front Foot Side Shift

From a front stance, move your front foot across in front of your body, reestablishing the feet at a 90-degree angle, perpendicular to each other with the legs in an X shape. The amount of weight on your front foot can vary from 20–90 percent, depending on the application.

Figure 9-4: Front foot side shift

Back Foot Side Shift

From a front stance, slide your back foot behind your front foot, creating an X shape with your legs. In the end, 90 percent of your weight will be on your front foot, with your back foot—only the toes and ball of the foot touching the ground—simply helping to maintain balance.

Training Tips

Watch the orientation of your feet. At the conclusion of all of these shifts, your feet should be more or less perpendicular to each other. That is, the toes of your back foot will be pointing at the heel of your front foot. Be sure your upper body remains centered and stable; you should not lean much in any direction.

KICKS ARE POWERFUL and extremely valuable; at the same time, they are more difficult to train for than hand and arm techniques. Thus, as a beginner, you are well advised to give careful attention to developing the leg muscles, balance, and coordination necessary for good kicking technique.

The Value of Kicks

Kicks are particularly valuable in fighting situations for two reasons. First, they can deliver a lot of power. The thigh muscle is the largest in the body; when its pure strength is coupled with torque and momentum from coordination with the whole body, the effect delivered through the foot (or knee) can be devastating. Second, kicks are of value because they increase the range of your attack without bringing you closer to your opponent. Your arms are relatively short, so to punch a target farther away, you have to move closer, which brings your body (and vital organs) into danger. But with a kick, you can remain at a

> **"T**he hands are like two swinging doors; rely on the legs for striking."

手是兩扇門，全憑腳打人

distance and still hit the target. A traditional Chinese saying captures the essence of the relationship and relative usefulness of arms and legs in a conflict as follows: "The hands are like two swinging doors; everything relies on the legs for hitting." The hands can deflect an attack and batter an opponent, like swinging café or saloon doors that can catch someone between them—but it's a kick that really has power.

The Risks of Kicks

But there is considerable risk in kicking. Another Chinese phrase warns of this: "Extending your leg (that is, executing a kick) is three degrees of danger (30 percent dangerous)." The reasons are perhaps obvious. When you kick, you have only one leg on the ground; therefore, you are more unstable. An opponent who sees this will try to take advantage of it and topple you. Falling/losing balance is perhaps the worst thing that can happen to you in a fight, because you are then not only vulnerable but also less able to counter or launch your own effective attack. Similarly, if your opponent grabs your foot when you kick, your means of defense or counterattack are limited. Your hands are probably too far away to be effective, your body is unstable, and you have little leverage or power to maneuver. A second reason kicking is risky for the kicker is the relatively long period of time (compared to a punch) a kick takes. If the opponent sees your kick coming, he or she has quite a bit of time to maneuver—to deflect your kick, to move out of the way, and the like—but you are totally committed to this maneuver until you finish it.

"**E**xtending your leg endangers yourself 30 percent." In other words, when you kick, in three out of ten cases you will get in trouble.

出 脚 三 分 險

The risks of kicking have two implications. First, you must train your kicks well. Give attention to training the *nonkicking* leg as much as the kicking leg. Balance and coordination are critical to a successful kick. The nonkicking leg must be steady as a rock and as firmly rooted to the ground as a tree, giving a solid base from which to launch your attack. You must be able to deliver a powerful kick and continue fighting without losing balance or focus. Speed is also critical. Ideally, the kick should come—and go—without the opponent knowing what hit him or her. You must prepare the kick without obvious warning, deliver it, and then withdraw the leg or foot immediately, as soon as the kick is completed.

The second implication of the danger of kicking is that you should use these techniques wisely. Do not take unnecessary risks. In any situation use the kick with the least danger to yourself. That is, don't launch a high kick when a swift, low kick will do; don't twist your body to deliver a dramatic side kick when a simple front snap will accomplish your purpose.

Training

In general, training legs is more difficult than training arms and hands. Note that, in stretching and warming up, it is the legs that require and receive the most attention. Arms are relatively easy to warm up because they are smaller, perhaps because they are anatomically more flexible, and because they do not bear weight.

In training kicks beginners should first work on balance and proper technique. Make sure you are kicking correctly, particularly in the way you use your knee, lower leg, and foot. Make sure you can hold your balance before, during, and after the kick. That is, you should be able to kick and withdraw your foot deliberately—either quickly or slowly—without falling. A good drill is to kick in slow motion or to stop the kick at various points during delivery (that is, hold the position just before you kick, at the height of the kick, and then after you withdraw your foot). Exercising in this way will help you develop control, balance, and strong essential muscles in both the kicking and nonkicking legs. After you have achieved good balance with proper technique,

In training kicks first work on balance and proper technique; then increase accuracy; finally, develop power and speed.

then try to increase accuracy. Whether high or low, front, side, or back, aim and try to place your kick precisely. The last elements to develop are speed and power. Only after you are certain you are performing the kicks correctly, smoothly, and accurately, *then* try to increase power and speed. Indeed, once you have developed the muscles and rhythm of the kick, these last two qualities—power and speed—will come almost naturally.

Since all kicks use the hip and knee and, to a lesser extent, the ankle, it is wise and useful to strengthen the muscles around all these joints. You may use light weights and any appropriate and safe exercises.

Finally, you can practice any kick as a drill. Assume any stance, then kick; the forward stance is particularly popular for this. Move back and forth, repeating the kick. Then switch, and practice with the other foot. Go slowly at first. Pause each time you return to the stance, and mentally check to be sure your arms, legs, and spine are in the correct position. As you kick, check to make sure your foot is oriented properly. Make sure your balance is solid and steady. Experiment with kicking high and low. Observe your body dynamics, and experiment with weight distribution to involve your entire body in delivering the kick. Develop a rhythm. By going slowly and checking yourself constantly, you will gradually build the specific muscles needed for each kick. At the same time you will be training your mind to focus and concentrate. Both are extremely valuable.

General Principles

Before learning specific kicks, give attention to these general principles:

✦ You can deliver any kick starting from any stance.

✦ From any stance you can kick with either foot.

✦ Any kick can be delivered high or low, from the ground, or in the air as a jump kick (except the low kick, which is necessarily low; it too can be delivered with a low jump).

✦ Keep your balance at all times; that is, maintain control before, during, and after the kick. Generally this means you must keep your weight centered over the foot on the ground. Maintaining a stable center enables you to kick with more power and ensures that you will be able to maintain the momentum of the fight (or the form) without a break.

✦ The nonkicking leg also participates in the kick. The leg on the ground not only acts as the "launching pad" for the kick, but also contributes power and spring, helping to increase the thrust of the kick. Therefore, in training, pay attention to the involvement and coordination of both legs.

Four Basic Kicks

The following notes describe in detail four basic kicks that are common to most styles of kung fu. Other kicks will be mentioned briefly, but the dynamics of kicking and the details of the many variations in the many styles—especially with regard to applications—make it almost impossible to describe advanced kicks adequately in words. All kicks, in fact, are probably best learned from an instructor by demonstration.

Front Snap, or Groin, Kick

This is a straightforward and basic kick, using the top of the foot as the striking surface. The target for this kick is usually the groin. In learning and practicing this kick, beginners should start to understand the complex coordination necessary between upper and lower body and between the two legs in order to execute a fast, accurate, and powerful kick without losing balance.

Basic kicks:

1. Front snap, or groin, kick

2. Low kick

3. Heel, or thrust, kick

4. Side kick

Figure 10-1: Front snap kick

Execution

The front snap kick can be executed moving forward or moving backward (retreating); it can be executed with either foot and from any stance. Shift the weight to your nonkicking leg, then lift the knee of your kicking leg. Bring the lower leg forward, and finally snap the foot out. Keep your kicking foot flexed back at the ankle, so that you use the top of the foot to hit the target (the groin of the opponent).

For a forward-moving front snap kick, shift your weight to your front leg, and kick with your back foot. For a retreating front snap kick, shift your weight to your back leg, and raise your front knee. Then snap out the foot of your front leg.

Training Tips

The most critical point—and most common error—is in the use of the knee. The kick should "snap" out from the knee, not swing out from the hip. Beginners tend to keep their knees locked and swing the whole leg as though the foot were a weight on the end of a stick; don't do this. The power should come from using both the hip and knee joints, not only the hip joint. Kicking with the whole leg takes longer, and your opponent can predict (see) your kick well in advance, which gives him or her the opportunity to counter.

The second point is that, as soon as you complete the kick, you should immediately pull your lower leg back—that is, snap your foot out from the knee, and then bring it back just as fast. This prevents your opponent from grabbing your foot, and it enables you to quickly kick again, if it seems appropriate.

The final point for beginners is to be careful when you first begin to practice this kick. Do not snap too hard, because the power and shock can damage your knee. Instead, execute the movement slowly and deliberately, gradually developing the supporting muscles around the knee. Later, when your knee is strong, then increase speed and power.

Low Kick

This is a kick to the knee or below—that is, to different sides of the knee, to the shin, or to the ankle. It is considered a popular and fun kick, especially among beginners, because it can be used from almost any direction (front, back, side, angled), and it's fast, easy to learn, and easy to apply. It doesn't require good balance or a difficult stance. Furthermore, it is less dangerous to the kicker—it does not expose him or her to attack from an opponent—but it can be devastat-

Figure 10-2: Low kick

ing to an opponent, especially when used to attack the knee. A kick to the front of the knee (to the kneecap) can disable an opponent; a kick to either side of the knee can break the leg, while a kick to the back of the knee will cause your opponent to fall.

Execution

The low kick is as simple as it is versatile. It can be executed moving forward or backward; it can be used to kick directly or at an angle; it can be executed with either foot and from any stance. Furthermore, you can use the inside or outside edge of the foot, the heel, or the toes to contact the opponent.

For a simple forward front low kick, shift your weight onto your nonkicking leg, lift and bring forward your kicking knee, and snap your foot out. This is the same as for a front snap kick, the difference being that you aim low for the low kick. The target should be the knee or some point below, either on the shin or the ankle.

For a back low kick, you aim to kick a target directly behind you with your heel. To execute this version of the low kick, lift the lower leg—but avoid raising your knee too high or too far forward—then thrust the leg out backward. Keep your foot flexed toward the shin so that power is sent to and through the heel.

For angled low kicks, reposition the nonkicking foot in the direction you wish to kick, then execute a kick.

Training Tips

This is a good kick for beginners to practice in order to develop balance and coordination for other, more difficult kicks. As with the front snap kick, be sure to bend your knee and use both hip and knee joints in delivering the kick; do not simply swing your leg.

Heel (Thrust) Kick

Compared to the front snap kick, the thrust kick is slower but far more power-ful. Indeed, this is probably the most powerful of the kicks, because it is so direct and because the strength of both legs as well as the body can be focused through the heel of the kicking foot. For example, this is the sort of kick that police officers use to break down doors. A front snap could never break down a door, because it mostly relies on the power of the leg alone and because the toes are not strong enough to deliver a powerful blow.

Heel kicks can be used to attack low or high targets, even the throat, accord-ing to the flexibility of the kicker.

Figure 10-3: Heel (thrust) kick

Execution

To execute a thrust kick, first transfer your weight to the nonkicking leg, and bend that knee, as though prepar-ing to spring. Lift the knee of the kicking leg, ankle cocked, then "thrust" it outward so that the heel strikes the target. As the kicking leg extends, the nonkicking leg also straightens, adding to the thrust. (The coordination of the two legs is critical; this can easily be seen in a demon-stration and must be developed in order to perform the kick correctly.)

Training Tips

The hip joint must be only partially open. If closed—that is, if both legs are pointed forward—it limits the height of the kick, simply as a result of the structure of the body. (You can see this yourself by experiment. Try delivering a kick with the toes pointed inward; then try again with the toes pointed outward.) However, if the joint is completely open, the kick is weaker. When the leg on the ground is pointed slightly outward, the kicking leg is said to be able to "borrow power" from the opposite leg to enhance the kick.

Don't worry about or try to control the orientation of your back (straight up, leaning forward or backward). Concentrate instead on keeping your balance and delivering a strong kick. Your back will automatically assume the position needed to support this delivery.

Side Kick

This is one of the strongest kicks available in the kung fu repertory, even potentially stronger than the heel thrust. In this kick the outside edge of the foot is used like a knife edge. Usually the hip joint is partially open (spread). The kick can go high or low. It can be directed at the shin, knee, kidney, rib, or waist of an opponent.

Figure 10-4: Side kick

The power of the side kick comes with one critical disadvantage: once completed, it leaves you almost completely exposed. Thus, it is to be used only when you have absolute confidence that it will completely finish your opponent.

Execution

In this kick your body faces forward while the kick is executed to the side, with the outside edge of the kicking foot leading. The toes of your nonkicking leg should start at approximately a 45-degree angle to the target ahead. Raise your knee, keeping the ankle cocked and the outside of the foot extended and leading. Strike out at a 90-degree angle. As your kicking foot snaps out, the foot on the ground shifts slightly, pivoting on the ball and positioning the heel in the direction of the kick as it supports the forward thrust of the kick. The snapping foot should be oriented with the outer edge aimed at the target and with the toes down and directed back toward your body as much as possible. Your body will naturally lean so that your upper arm is extended parallel to the kicking leg and the ground.

Other Kicks

Arrow Kick

This is exactly like the groin kick, except in the position of the foot/toes of the kicking foot. In this case the toes of the foot should shoot out like an arrow from a bow, directly at the target. As your knee rises, keep the foot cocked (at a right angle to the lower leg). When the knee thrusts the lower leg out, the foot straightens, thrusting the toes into the target—which can be high (for example, the throat) or low (for example, the diaphragm, the solar plexus).

Crescent Kicks

Crescent kicks are essentially circular kicks, using the whole leg as a unit. All of these kicks require very open hip joints, allowing the leg full range of movement within the socket. Build this flexibility gradually. Especially at first, do not practice too many of these kicks too vigorously; otherwise you risk strain and sprain, if not damage.

Inside Crescent Kick

This kick uses the whole inner side of the leg for kicking; the target would be the back of the opponent's head or the kidney. For a right kick, support your

Figure 10-5: Arrow kick

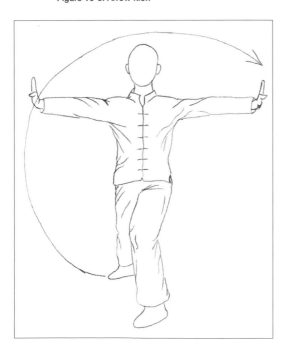

weight on your left leg, and swing your right leg in a counter-clockwise arc—out to the right, then up, to the left, and down again. Do not lock the knee. In the beginning simply try to make the kick as smooth and circular as possible; relax and allow your leg to swing. As the kick gets looser and faster, then work on getting a broader, higher sweep with more power.

Figure 10-6: Inside crescent kick using right foot

Figure 10-7: Outside crescent kick using left foot

Figure 10-8: Roundhouse kick, first part

Outside Crescent Kick

This kick is exactly like the inside crescent kick except that the leg sweeps up then out, rather than up and in. (For a right kick, this means clockwise.) Again, first work on a smooth, easy motion, then develop speed, height, and power. Keep the kicking leg straight, but do not lock the knee.

Roundhouse Kick

This open-ankle kick carries an element of surprise as well as force. It is as strong as a side kick, which it resembles in direction of attack, and it can be used to strike high (head, throat), middle (kidney), or low (knee) targets. It is usually used to attack targets from behind.

In this kick your body faces about 45 degrees between front and side; your nonkicking leg is forward. Raise the knee of the back, kicking leg and sweep it in a semicircle around from behind, then snap out your lower leg. You may strike the target with either the top of your ankle (in which case, keep your ankle open as you raise your knee) or the ball of your foot (in which case, keep your toes pointed backward toward the leg).

The roundhouse kick resembles the side kick in that it is

not delivered facing the target directly, but it differs in that the kicking leg sweeps around from behind rather than simply rising at the side of the body. Proper execution requires an open hip and flexible waist, as well as strong knees and ankles.

Figure 10-9: Roundhouse kick, second part

chapter 11
hand techniques

YOUR ARMS—from shoulder to hands—are the fastest, most versatile, and most readily available natural weapons you have. Used for both attack and defense, fists, hands, and arms can block, trap, punch, deflect, grab, claw, push, and jab, to name a few possibilities. Many styles of kung fu have distinct hand and fist forms—such as the tiger claw in the *Fu Jow Pai* style and mantis hand in the Praying Mantis style. Achieving full benefit from hand and arm techniques requires careful attention to the relationship of hand to arm to body, as well as rigorous training in speed, strength, accuracy, and flexibility.

Handiness

In general, hands and arms are the first line of defense in protecting the body. Note that, in most martial arts, including wrestling and boxing, the natural "on guard" position is one in which both hands are poised in front of the body, prepared to protect or launch an attack at the first opportunity. This is naturally good technique. Hands and arms are easier to control than feet. The arm in the shoulder socket has almost 360 degrees of natural motion, plus the capability of rotation; similarly, the elbow and wrist can rotate and turn,

The speed and versatility of hands and arms make them the first line of defense in protecting the body.

increasing the capability of the arm as a whole. Furthermore, arms are faster than feet, and both can move at the same time. As a result of these characteristics, hands have many more options than feet, both in the postures they can assume and in how they move in both attacking and defending. Hands may be used straight, clenched, or partially clenched (claw); they may be used to attack (punch, jab, grab, claw), to deflect an incoming punch or kick (block, guide), or to trap or lock joints. The forearm can be used to block in various orientations, as can the upper arm. And then the elbow can be used to strike, as can the shoulder. The combinations are endless.

The legs, in contrast, are limited by their size, anatomy, and essential function of supporting the body. One foot must be on the ground at all times, preferably firmly rooted, so usually only one leg can be used for other purposes. The ankle, knee, and hip are necessarily less free and flexible than their arm counterparts because they bear the body's weight.

Fundamental Concepts

Training the arms is generally easier than training the legs. Nevertheless, you need to understand certain fundamental concepts to ensure that you have the right goal in mind and therefore train properly and effectively.

1. Speed beats power. A traditional martial arts saying counsels, "There is no technique that you cannot overcome (that is, no technique is 100 percent effective), but speed cannot be overcome (there is no defense/counterattack against speed)." The common sense of this is clear. If an opponent attacks so quickly that you cannot respond, you lose. Therefore, in training never sacrifice speed for power. Do not develop your muscles at the sacrifice of agility and flexibility. If you do so, then you may be able to knock a punching bag or lift heavy weights, but the strength is not likely to be useful to you in a sparring or fighting situation.

2. Deliver full power to the endpoint. In kung fu, the goal is to deliver full force to the target. The arm may be strong throughout its length, but in delivering a punch, the goal is to focus all power in the fist at the moment it reaches the target. Consider a comparison between striking a target with a 100-pound iron bar and striking it with a 100-pound weight on the end of a chain. Which will have a stronger impact? The iron will have less impact because its strength is distributed throughout its length. For some purposes this is valuable, but if you strike a target with the bar, only a small amount of its force is delivered to the point of contact. In contrast, with a weight on a chain, the striking force is far greater because all of the weight is delivered to the endpoint.

The human arm can function either like an iron bar or like a chain with a weight on the end. The difference comes from how the arm is used and the intention guiding its use. Thus, there are two important elements in training: physical and mental. After understanding the goal, by concentration and repeated practice you will learn how to achieve it.

Sending power to the end of the arm requires that the rest of the arm be relaxed and loose. In this way no energy is wasted in muscle tension;

By relaxing the arm full power can be delivered through the fist.

a relaxed arm will transmit the energy quickly and completely to the end. To achieve this, you must first train the muscles to relax and move smoothly; then you train to deliver power. It takes time. Gradually you will understand the concept and how to do it. This can only be achieved through practice and attention, ideally with the help of an instructor.

This ancient poem describes the way of delivering explosive power to the fist:

"Hand [technique] is divided into three:
First, loosen the shoulder.
Second, sink the elbow.
Third, a wild tiger emerges from the jungle."

鬆肩，沉肘．猛虎出林．

3. Circling conserves energy (power). The beginning kung fu student may see that many of the hand and arm movements flow in circles, with either one or both hands, moving clockwise or counterclockwise. This circular motion conserves energy and enables smooth transitions from one movement to another, according to need and strategy. The original

form of this concept is attributed to a General Yue Fei, who trained his soldiers in this technique to fight the army of Genghis Khan, and it is characterized, in Chinese, as "The pushing hands of General Yue." In the movie *Karate Kid*, Mr. Miyagi trained Daniel-san with similar exercises: "wax on" with a clockwise circular motion of the right hand, then "wax off" with a circular motion of the left hand. The idea is to keep the energy flowing smoothly and continuously, so that it is available instantly and fully for any purpose. In the many different styles of kung fu, the details may differ—hand formation, size of circle, direction of circle, one hand going one way and the other the opposite, the hands making motions of different sizes—but the concept is the same.

Training

For drills use any type of stance—but use *some* good stance—then practice your punches. Front stance is probably the best for this purpose, as it tends to support the weight and the forward thrust of the punch, and it also helps the waist to turn.

Some styles train first with one hand, then the other hand, then both hands; training in this way tends to produce better results. This approach is particularly good if the movements seem awkward or strange to you or if you are having trouble in any way.

Hand Techniques

The most common hand techniques found in both northern and southern styles of kung fu are described below. The list is by no means complete because each style has variations, and more advanced techniques (such as chin-na, or joint locking) are not mentioned. Mastery of the following should be enough for beginning levels.

Open Hand
Willow Leaf Palm

This is the typical open-handed form of northern styles of kung fu. The four fingers are kept straight, tightly pressed together, with the thumb cocked, tucked firmly against the palm. The wrist is slightly bent, except for piercing, in which case it is held straight. (In Japanese martial arts, this is known as the "knife hand.")

Figure 11-1: Willow leaf palm

The willow leaf palm or hand can be used in five ways. Both the inside and outside edges of the palm can be used to strike; the heel of the hand can be used; the whole hand can be used in a front thrust to pierce; and the flat of the back of the hand can be used to strike. Thus, the open hand is a particularly flexible, fast, and versatile natural weapon for any kung fu artist.

Tiger Palm

Southern styles of kung fu use a slight variation of the willow leaf, the tiger palm, as their open-hand form. In the tiger palm, the four fingers and thumb are kept slightly bent and slightly separated. Note

Figure 11-2: Tiger palm

that to achieve the characteristic appearance, only the finger joints are slightly bent—the knuckles are flat, so that the basal bones of the fingers are even, or level, with the tendons in the hand.

The tiger palm can be used in all the ways that the willow leaf can, plus one: the tiger palm can be used as a claw or grab.

Finger Thrust

Use (1) index finger alone, (2) two fingers (index and middle fingers) held together or held apart, or (3) four fingers together. This technique is used with a thrusting motion, to the throat, to the eyes, or to vital points. In sparring it should be used only with great care; indeed, in some schools it is forbidden because it is so dangerous, especially for beginners who lack control and for women who have long fingernails. When you use this thrust in sparring, your fingers should always be kept curled to make sure you don't hurt your partner.

Fists

The closed-hand flat fist is probably the most basic hand form for any style of fighting, kung fu included. For the kung fu fist, close the four fingers into the palm—but do not clench your fist. The knuckles of the four fingers should form a flat surface, perpendicular to the line of your arm. If you tightly clench your fist, the surface of the knuckles will be slanted in relation to your arm. Fold your thumb over the fingers, keeping it bent so that the tip of the thumb does not protrude beyond your knuckles; it should be completely below or behind the knuckles. Your wrist must be straight, not bent in either direction. The best way to check the form of your wrist is to press your fist against a hard surface, as though punching, or to do pushups with your fists on the ground instead of your open palms. The knuckles should all line up against the surface, and your wrist should enable you to deliver full force from your shoulder through your knuckles. This is the strongest and safest fist for punching.

Horizontal

For a horizontal fist/punch, the top of the knuckles are uppermost, with the palm facing downward.

Vertical

For a vertical fist/punch, the thumb-side of the hand is uppermost, with the knuckles facing outward. (For example, in a vertical punch with the right hand, the knuckles are pointing to the right, the palm of the hand to the left.)

Figure 11-3: Horizontal fist

Figure 11-4: Vertical fist

Figure 11-5: Tiger claw

Figure 11-6: Eagle claw

Claws

Tiger Claw

This is a southern-style hand formation with many applications. As the name suggests, the tiger claw is a more extreme version of the tiger palm. As in the tiger palm, the finger and thumb joints are bent—in this case almost at right angles—and the fingers and thumb are held slightly separated. The hand can be held either even with the forearm, bent upward, or bent downward, depending on the application. If the hand is bent up, the heel can be used to strike; when used to grab an opponent's arm, for example, the claw hand will revolve and be bent forward. When using the edge of the claw, the hand would most likely be held straight. In any case, the entire hand should be locked into position.

To get the correct orientation of your fingers in the fist, do a knuckle push-up against the floor or a wall.

Eagle Claw

The eagle claw, which is common to both northern and southern styles, resembles the tiger claw in the shape and tension of the fingers; it differs in that, here, the fingers are held together, and the hand is held bent back. In both tiger and eagle claws, the thumb is bent and held off to the side of the hand. The

> To develop finger strength for the eagle claw, lift wide-mouth jars filled with sand or water.

eagle claw is very effective for gripping, for chin-na grabbing and locking, and for accessing vital points.

Mantis Claw or Cranesbeak

Most schools of both northern and southern kung fu have a hand form of this type; the Praying Mantis schools call it the "mantis claw," while some other northern schools and southern schools call it the "cranesbeak." To make it, start

Figure 11-7: Mantis claw

with an open hand with relaxed, spread fingers. Curl the fingers into your palm, one by one in succession, starting with the smallest finger and ending with the thumb; your index finger sometimes remains straight and pointed somewhat outward. Then curl your wrist downward. In the finished position, your fingers will be curled and pressed together, with the index finger slightly extended and the thumb pressed against it. The principle of this hand position is to grab the arm or wrist of an opponent, without locking your fingers around the limb. In this way you have contact with ("sticking to") the opponent, so you can guide or sense his or her next move; without the total commitment of a grab, however, you can also easily release your opponent.

Arm Strikes

Straight Punch

Your fist can be either vertical or horizontal. Punch directly forward. Having reached full extension, your fist should then bounce or spring back a little. That is, after delivering the punch, your arm should return to a somewhat elastic, relaxed, and alert resting position. Never lock your elbow. (In some specific punches of some styles, the thumb may be in a slightly different position. Pay attention to this detail in any demonstrations at your school.)

Backfist

In this technique the back of the fist is used to strike with leverage from the elbow. There are three types: horizontal (or side), vertical, and angled (slightly upward or downward). To execute a backfist, make a fist, then bend your elbow, holding your forearm horizontally in front of your chest. For the side backfist, swing your arm to the side from the elbow, striking the target with the back of your fist. For the traditional, vertical backfist, from the position described above, using your elbow as a fulcrum, twirl your forearm in toward your chest, then upward and out, striking the target with the back side (knuckles) of your fist. Thus, your elbow remains in more or less the same position, as your forearm spins and gathers momentum for the strike. For an angled backfist, swing your forearm either upward or downward, depending on the target.

Figure 11-8: Backfist

Hook

The arm, fully extended, swings in an arc, first out to the side and then up and across your body, ending at the opposite shoulder. The target could be either high (the head, for example) or low (the kidneys, for example). Your fingers should make a fist; your knuckles may lead or follow, depending on the style. Never lock your elbow.

Figure 11-9: Hook strike

Uppercut

From a position at the side of your body, with the fingers in a fist, knuckles down and palm up, your arm swings up, delivering a rising blow either to the chin or the diaphragm of your opponent. In a short uppercut, your arm is bent and begins at the waist. In a long uppercut, your arm begins, fully extended, at your side.

Figure 11-10: Uppercut

Blocks

Circular Block

For circular blocks of all description, the arm moves in a circle in front of the body, thus using full arm strength to deflect an incoming blow. The hand can be in any position. These are the original methods of General Yue Fei (as described in the introduction to this chapter).

Outside

For an outside circular block, the forearm first circles up in front of your body, and then outward. For example, on the right side, your right arm would move in a clockwise direction, ending with your hand at head height.

Inside

For an inside circular block, the forearm travels down across your body from an upper to lower position. On the right side, your right arm would move in a counterclockwise direction, from upper right across the front of your body and back to lower right.

Combination

In a combination block, both arms work together. As your right arm goes out, the left moves in, so both arms are moving in a clockwise direction. Or, as your left arm goes out, the right can move in, both arcing in a counterclockwise direction.

Figure 11-11: Straight cut or down block

Straight Cut or Down Block

In this move the forearm moves from an upper position on its side of the body, diagonally down across the front of the body to the opposite lower side. The starting height can be at your head or shoulder. Your hand is usually held as a fist or flat palm. In practicing, the other arm often swings across your body in an opposite action to counterbalance the block and to position itself defensively, ready to strike. For example, for a right down block, your arm would move from upper right to lower left.

Figure 11-12: Lift or upper block

Lift or Upper Block

In this move the forearm moves from its side of the body, diagonally up across the body, with the outside of the arm leading. Start with your arm extended or bent at the waist, and then thrust your forearm upward. For a right upper block, your arm would move from lower right to the center or upper left, depending on the target.

Intercepting Block

In this move your arm is bent at a right angle at the elbow and held in this position as it moves across the front of your body. A right intercepting block would move from right to left. The hand is usually held as a fist or open palm.

Figure 11-13: Intercepting block

Cross Down Block

In this technique, your arm moves from an upper position at the opposite shoulder, diagonally down across the front of your body, back to a lower position on its side of the body. That is, for a right cross down block, your arm would move from upper left to lower right.

Elbow Strikes

For an elbow strike the elbow is bent, bringing the hand back to the shoulder. With leverage from the shoulder, the elbow can be used to deliver powerful blows.

Front

The elbow moves horizontally from outside toward the center of the body. That is, for an elbow strike with your right arm, your elbow would move from right to left, ending more or less at the center of your body.

Figure 11-14: Cross down block

This phrase expresses an important, if enigmatic, principle of kung fu. A direct translation would be, "Circles among circles, search inside the circle." It suggests that the effectiveness of strategy and technique in kung fu lies in using the unique properties of circular motion.

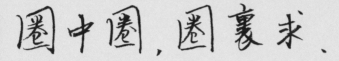

Straight

The elbow moves vertically, upward and in a straight line. The more open and flexible the shoulder, the farther the strike can travel.

Side

The elbow moves horizontally from a position at the center of the body toward the outside. Generally, to execute a side elbow strike, the elbow moves in an arc from a position at the side upward and then across the body into position

Figure 11-15: Side elbow strike

for the sweep to the side. That is, for a side elbow strike with your right arm, in most applications your elbow would move up and to the left, then sweep down and to the right in the strike.

Back

The back elbow strike resembles the side elbow strike, in that the elbow travels horizontally from a position near the center of the body outward; in this case, however, the waist turns so that the elbow travels around the side of the body to the back. In executing this strike, you must be careful not to swing your elbow with such force that you lose balance. This will give your opponent the advantage and enable him or her to use your power against you.

Outlatch

The outlatch is a circular movement of one arm sweeping up and out past the other arm. It is strictly a transition movement, executed to switch your hands in preparation for a punch, grab, or other maneuver. While there are many variations, in a typical outlatch, after one arm blocks an incoming punch, your other arm then sweeps up along the outside of your first arm, pushing your opponent's punching arm to the side and releasing your first arm for a grab, punch, or the like.

practice

THE SIX CHAPTERS of this section cover aspects of ongoing training. Virtually every workout will comprise four or five elements: warming up, drills and conditioning exercises, forms, (sparring) and cooling down. In addition, pervading the whole is the aspect of mental awareness, or internal training. Each is important; none can be omitted.

Warming up ensures that your body is in peak condition for the work ahead; it also goes a long way toward preventing injury. Drills and conditioning exercises build strength, increase endurance, improve balance, and allow you to focus on overcoming specific weaknesses. Doing forms challenges your mind and improves your coordination, flexibility, and fluidity. Throughout it all, maintaining alertness, concentration, focus, and determination is part of the essential mental or internal aspects of your training. Finally, there are a few words on safety to help you get the most benefit with the least injury or discomfort.

Altogether, you are developing body, mind, and spirit.

warming up

WARM-UP AND COOL-DOWN sessions typically begin and end workout sessions in any kung fu school and serve important purposes. By warming your body and loosening your joints before you begin vigorous movement, you prevent injury and help your body perform at its best for a longer period of time. By stretching your muscles you increase their flexibility, strength, and endurance. By clearing and settling your mind, you prepare it, too, to work efficiently. In reverse, at the end of the workout, the cool-down session gradually brings body and mind back to a calm state. Gentle exercise prevents blood from pooling,

Warming up is like creating nice weather inside your body: When you feel good, you'll work harder and enjoy it more.

which can happen when exercise stops suddenly, and which can cause dizziness. Stretching at this time gets a bit more length from thoroughly warmed tissues. Both warm-up and cool-down sessions are valuable components of your training.

Your School's Style

Every school and/or sifu will have its/his/her own style or method for warming up/cooling down. In larger schools with fixed and limited times for practice, as well as limited space, there will probably be group sessions. Such sessions typically comprise, to begin, a series of loosening and stretching exercises, followed by practice in some of the basic stances, punches, and kicks.

Cool-down sessions typically comprise gentle exercises and a short meditation, or mind-centering sitting period.

In smaller schools, where students may come and go over a two- to three-hour period, both warming up and cooling down may be left to the student. In this case the instructor may teach you some exercises or make suggestions, but will essentially leave the style and length of your warm-up session to you. You may follow your own routine or copy the routine of older students. (If you have any questions or need any guidance, be sure to ask the Chief Instructor or any of the senior students; they should be more than happy to help.)

Find a warm-up style you like and stick with it.

Advanced students of kung fu sometimes use a simple form—especially one of the beginning forms—as a warm-up. Some of these forms sufficiently stretch and flex the body to serve this purpose and are more interesting for some people than calisthenics-like drills. Find what works best for you and develop it, to keep pace with your own development.

Principles in Practice

The principles and purpose of the warm-up/cool-down sessions are basically the same for kung fu as for any other sport or athletic exercise, at least at the beginning level. Thus, you may follow any routine and use any exercises that accomplish those purposes, whether they come from yoga, calisthenics, your local health club, or a fitness magazine. The following are some general principles to apply and some general warnings as to what to avoid.

Warm the Body

The first goal is to stimulate blood circulation to get the body warm. Do some gentle movements that will get your heart pumping a little faster, expand the blood vessels, and activate the muscles. Begin with slow, small movements and gradually increase the range of motion, speed, and intensity. When you feel your skin growing warm and beginning to sweat, you are ready to move on.

This warming phase usually takes four to five minutes, probably longer during cold weather and for people who are less fit. Don't cheat yourself; take the time you need to make sure your body is ready.

Flex

The second goal is to loosen the joints. These exercises can be part of warming the body; you may work either from the smaller joints to the larger joints, or from the top of your body downward. Keep your muscles relaxed throughout, so that the joints are free to move.

One approach to loosening the joints is to use gentle shaking or bouncing movements. Start with your wrists, elbows, and shoulders, shaking them freely. Then bounce your entire body, loosely, up and down.

A second approach is to use circular motions throughout. For example, clasp your hands together, and then rotate them together at the wrist, first clockwise, then counterclockwise. For your ankles, put the weight on one foot, lift the other so that just the toe touches the ground, and then rotate the raised foot at the ankle. For your knees, squat slightly, put one hand on each knee, and then rotate the knees first in one direction and then the other. Finally, be sure your spine is loose and flexible—from neck to waist—by rotating your waist and twisting your torso. Pay particular attention to the waist, which will generate movement in the rest of the body.

> Loosening ligaments and opening joints, especially in the pelvis and hips, are important before doing vigorous kicks, to avoid injury to your lower back.

When you finish, your wrists and ankles, knees and elbows, shoulders and hips should all be moving smoothly in the full range of their motion. The alignment of these three pairs of joints is known as the "six harmonies" and is fundamental to generating power, maintaining balance, and developing effective technique. Loosening them helps you achieve the proper posture and harmonious alignment of these joints.

Stretch

Third, stretch. Stretching elongates the muscles, allowing greater range of motion (which means greater flexibility) and stronger power. Both are critical components of kung fu. It is said that rigorous stretching exercises were the first stage in the Shaolin monks' daily training routine. Even today, dedicated kung fu practitioners stretch daily in order to maintain flexibility and good muscle condition. Stretching is best done both before and after the workout; that is, light stretching first and more concentrated stretching after. After the workout, because your muscles are thoroughly warm, you can be more confident that you will not cause injury, and you can get greater effect from your efforts. In any case, go slow and work gradually.

> **Y**ou will improve faster if you take it easy: stretch thoroughly, but don't force anything.

There are many exercises for stretching, from both Western and Eastern disciplines (for example, toe touching, lotus position, various forward bends from standing and seated positions). Use the ones recommended by your sifu or practiced in your school, or use the ones that you have found by experience to be particularly effective. Whatever exercises you choose, keep the following general guidelines in mind for the best results:

1. Only stretch warm muscles. You may begin any workout with gentle stretches—like animals waking up after sleep—but for serious, concentrated stretching, only work on warm muscles. Otherwise you risk injury.

2. Only stretch relaxed muscles. Before you begin each stretch, relax—use your mind to target and relax each muscle as you begin the stretch. This will ensure that you get the full benefit and avoid injury from prolonged stretching.

3. Don't bounce. That is, stretch gently and slowly, with muscle control throughout. Bouncing can make the muscle move beyond its normal range of motion and cause strains and even damage.

4. Do not overstretch. Overstretching occurs when the muscle exceeds its normal range of motion and is the precursor to tears. Put tension on the muscle until you can feel the muscle stretching—but not until you feel pain. If it hurts, stop, because pain could be a signal that you are causing damage. It is especially important to stop if you feel pain in a joint, such as the knees or hips. If this occurs, first check your posture; if everything seems correct but the pain continues, you might want to seek the advice of a medical practitioner to make sure there is not a more serious problem in the making.

5. Breathe throughout the stretch. Fill your lungs; exhale as you stretch; this will increase the effectiveness of the stretch.

6. Maintain proper body alignment. This will ensure that your stretches target the correct muscle groups and that you do not cause injury. You may think of a vertical line going through your head and the center of your body and parallel horizontal lines through your shoulders and hips. Maintain this alignment as closely as possible for maximum grace as well as power. In other words, keep your hips square; do not twist or turn them to make the stretch easier. Use your spine properly. For example, in some forward bends, there should be a progressive bend from the bottom of the spine to the top: do not simply bend in the middle of the back. If there are mirrors in the school, use them to make sure you are stretching with good form.

7. Often, working on strength and flexibility together is a good idea. That is, begin some strength training at the same time as you start stretching routines. This ensures that the muscles are growing stronger as well as more flexible.

8. Work progressively, from easier stretches to more difficult stretches.

9. The most effective stretches are those that mimic the actions that you will be using in your sport or activity (that is, stretches that use the same muscles, joints, and so on, in the same way). Thus, isolated moves (stances, kicks, and punches) from the forms you are doing can be excellent stretching exercises.

10. Stretch intermittently. That is, maintain a stretch for twenty to thirty seconds, relax, then repeat. Continue this off-on procedure for several minutes. Some sifus recommend stretching each muscle for a minimum of four to five minutes.

Mind Helping Matter

In terms of your mind, the purposes of the warm-up session are to empty and focus. Sometimes a brief period of meditation begins the warm-up or concludes the cool-down session. Whether or not you specifically sit in meditation, you should take time to settle your mind and bring it into coordination with your body. This may be accomplished in two phases.

First, empty your mind of all that is not relevant to the tasks at hand. You have set aside this time for kung fu training, and any other cares or obligations or thoughts are not relevant or useful. Banish them until later.

Second, focus on what you are doing. Having created empty space in your mind, now allow awareness of your body and the challenge of kung fu training to fill it completely. Use this time of the warm-up session to move mentally from the outside world into this inner world of your body and the kung fu training. Participate in the warm-up session with as much attention and focus as you intend to give to the training sessions. This, too, is important practice.

Enjoy. That is the shortcut to coordinating mind and body.

As you move and stretch, give attention to each muscle group involved; be aware of what your body is doing, of its posture and alignment. Use your mind to help your muscles stretch and extend. By using your mind to support and enhance the physical aspects of the warm-up session, you will not only get the most out of the warm-up, but you will also prepare to get the most out of your entire training session.

As with all the other kung fu routines you will do, perform your warm-up and cool-down exercises conscientiously. The warm-up session should begin gently and gradually increase in intensity; it should exercise all parts of the body. Stay relaxed throughout. Clear your mind of unrelated thoughts, focus it on your body, and use it to increase the effectiveness of the exercises. Do not allow your mind to wander nor your movements to become sloppy.

Similarly, but in reverse, the cool-down should gradually bring your body back to a state of rest. A short meditation or period of contemplation should either begin the warm-up or end the cool-down session, or possibly both.

Sample Warmup Routine
First working from head to toe:

1. Loosen the upper body. Letting your arms hang limply, shake your wrists from side to side, or up and down, or in small circles.
2. Head. Rotate your head or bend your neck from side to side (see Figure 12-1). Use care when bending your neck backward; letting your head hang or drop backward could damage your neck because of the head's weight.

Figure 12-1: Head rolls

3. Shoulders. Roll your shoulders forward and backward in circles, or push them up and down, front to back, back to front.

4. Waist. Put your hands over your kidneys, with the palms against your lower back, fingers downward, and rotate your hips, clockwise then counterclockwise. Keep your feet together. This exercise massages the internal organs (liver, spleen, and so on).

5. Side stretch. Raise one arm over your head, palm facing forward, and place the other arm behind your back, with the back of your hand on the buttocks; bend gently to the side, stretching the overhead arm. Repeat on the other side.

6. Forward and back stretch. Keeping your back flat, bend forward and stretch your arms out to the front. Only bend forward to the level of your waist; that is, your body should be level and parallel to the ground with your arms in front. Then bend backward. Keep your eyes on your fingertips or on the ceiling; bend back only as far as is comfortable (if you force it, you could fall), until your chin points to the ceiling. Then bend back to the front, and repeat. (At advanced levels, you may rotate the upper body with arms outstretched, as above, first to the right then the left, in large circles.)

7. Hips. Put the palms of your hands on the back of your hip joint. Spread your legs a little farther than shoulders' width, and rotate your hips clockwise and then counterclockwise. (While this resembles Number 4 above, the effect is different: this exercises the hip joint.)

8. Hips and hamstring stretch. Starting from a forward stance (see Chapter 8), push your front leg forward, but only to the point that the knee of the front leg is over your toes—not beyond; keep the heel of your back foot on the ground. Hold for several seconds. Repeat on the other side.

Figure 12-2: Knee circles

9. Knees. With feet together and flat on the floor (don't let your heels rise), bend your knees and squat; then, with both hands resting on your knees, slowly rotate your knees together, first clockwise, then counterclockwise (see Figure 12-2).

10. Ankles. Stand with your feet shoulders' width apart. Move one foot slightly back, toe tip touching the ground (even with the heel of the opposite foot); rotate the foot, first in one direction, then the other. Repeat with your other foot.

...now working more vigorously:

11. Arm circles. Swing your arms in circles, using the full range of the shoulder joint, lightly, without force, but with even rhythm. First forward circles, then backward circles. You can circle both arms together in the same direction, or alternately, first one arm, then the other.

12. Upper torso rotation. Hold your arms bent at the elbows, level, in front of your chest, with your hands in fists, knuckles touching; turn to the right and left as far as is comfortable (do not force it); your legs and hips should remain facing front.

13. Thigh rotation. Stand with your feet spread. Shift your weight to one side, lift the other knee, keeping it bent to about waist height, and circle it from inside to outside. Set the foot down, approximately in starting position. Lift your other knee and repeat on the other side.

14. Knee strengthening and balance (forward). Stand with your feet shoulders' width apart, hands on hips; shift your weight to one leg and hold the other leg straight out in front. Squat slightly on the weight-bearing leg. Keep your back straight. Repeat several times, then repeat with your other leg.

15. Knee strengthening and balance (backward). Stand with your feet shoulders' width apart; lean forward, stretching your arms out in front (as though reaching for something), with one leg out in back. Holding your

balance, squat slightly on your supporting leg. Keep your back flat. Repeat several times, and then use the other leg.

16. Leg swing-kicks. Start with a loose forward stance. Hold your forward arm up at an angle forward, with your hand just above head height; hold your back arm to the back, loosely in line with the forward arm for balance. Bend the knee of your back leg, and snap your foot out in a gentle kick at knee height (no higher); let the foot be relaxed. Then swing the straight leg back, as though kicking behind. Then swing-kick forward. Repeat several times, with a swinging rhythm, to front and back. Repeat on the other side.

Stretches Particularly Useful for Kung fu

1. Forward bends. Stand with feet together, both hands together over your head, fingers laced together, palms outward. With back straight and knees loosely locked, lean forward, bringing your hands toward the ground. Do not strain or overdo it, especially at the beginning. The more you do, the warmer your muscles get, and the lower you will be able to

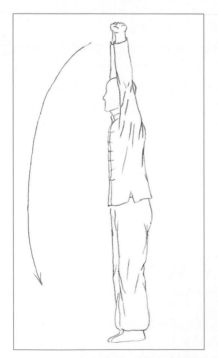

go. Stretching the backs of your legs will increase the vertical range of your kicks; this exercise also trims the waist and tightens the stomach.

2. Waist stretch and twist. This is a continuation of the above exercise. After you bend down and forward, turn 90 degrees to one side (see Figures 12-3 and 12-4), and try to bring your hands down to touch close to the outside of your ankle (see Figure 12-5). Rise slowly on the side, then turn to the front, bringing your hands back to the overhead position.

Again bend forward; this time, when your hands reach the ground, twist to the other side. When your hands reach your ankle, raise your arms on that side, slowly; when your hands are up, turn your body again to the front. This exercise particularly

Figure 12-3: Waist stretch and twist, first part

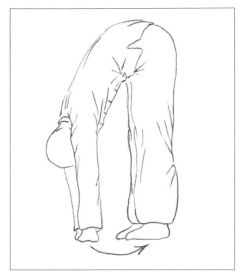

Figure 12-4: Waist stretch and twist, second part

Figure 12-5: Waist stretch and twist, third part

limbers the waist and facilitates the circular motion of kicks (crescent kicks, for example).

3. Leg stretch: Opposite toe/ankle touch. From spread-eagle position (feet spread, hands spread), extend one hand to the opposite toe or ankle, allowing your other arm to extend to the back. Right hand to left foot; left hand to right foot. Like the above, it limbers the waist, but in a slightly different way, thus further improving general performance.

4. Poke stance stretch. With feet widely spaced (well beyond shoulders' width), flat on the ground, and both pointing forward, squat over one leg. In the beginning don't go too low, and use your hands for support and balance (that is, place one hand on the floor between your legs, and one hand forward of your bent knee). Simply sit in this position. Then shift to the other side. Remain in the position on each side for several minutes. At first, you will not be able to go too low, and you may not be able to hold the position for too long, but keep practicing. Use your mind to help relax and stretch the muscles and tendons involved. Shift positions slowly and deliberately, in order to build strong knee muscles. The poke stance is common to most kung fu styles; developing the ability to get in and out of this position quickly, easily, and smoothly is well worthwhile.

Figure 12-6: Poke stance stretch

5. Crane stance and stretch. Stand in a crane stance; grasp the bottom of your raised foot with the opposite hand, and grasp the shin or knee of the raised leg with the arm on the same side (see Figure 12-7). Keeping your back erect, maintain this position. For further exercise, you may extend your raised leg until the knee is straight, and then

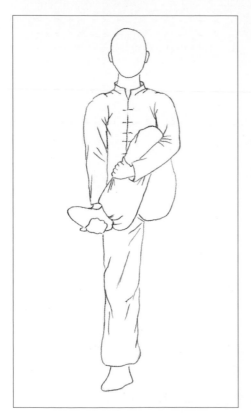

Figure 12-7: Crane stance and stretch, first part

Figure 12-8: Crane stance and stretch, second part

raise it as far as possible—keeping your hand on the bottom of your foot
(see Figure 12-8). Again, simply maintain this position. The purpose of
this exercise is to develop the muscles involved in the crane stance and
to improve balance.

chapter 13
participating in
a workout

DURING THE ORIENTATION SESSION, the instructors will probably explain how workouts are organized and what new students will need to know in terms of etiquette. At most schools group training sessions comprise specific elements: First, possibly, there is a salute to the instructors (see Figure 13-1). Then a warm-up. At that point, while the whole class is together, there may be a demonstration of new material for all students. Following the demonstration, the class may break up into smaller groups for work on new and previously learned material, for working with partners, for questions and clarifications, and so on. Or individuals may be left to practice on their own. At some point during the session, there are likely to be drills and/or opportunities for individuals to work on strength and endurance (work with the punching bag, weights, iron palm sandbag, and other equipment that may be in the school). Finally, as the end of the session draws near, the instructor may call everyone together for a cool-down session, and/or meditation, and/or salute to officially close the session.

Figure 13-1: The traditional kung fu salute, holding both hands poised in front of the body, right fist in left palm, with a slight bow of the upper body

The Four Components of Learning

"The four components of learning are explanation, demonstration, imitation, and repetition. The goal is to create a correct habit that can be produced instinctively under great pressure [at any time]."

This anonymous quotation summarizes precisely what is happening in a workout session. The goal is to teach correct forms—stances, punches, blocks, kicks, and the rest—that will become so ingrained that you will perform them spontaneously, correctly, and swiftly when needed. The time of "need" could be a real fight, a friendly sparring session, a public demonstration, or a tournament competition. You should know the patterns so well that you can do them no matter what temptations to distraction may occur—so well that you can do them in your sleep. (And indeed, some veteran students are known to punch and kick even in their dreams!)

> **The Four Components of a Workout Session**
>
> Explanation
>
> Demonstration
>
> Imitation
>
> Repetition

The method of producing these automatic habits—the four steps listed above—is part of every workout session. There will be explanation and demonstration; then there will be an opportunity for you to imitate. And then, once it seems you know what to do, you will be asked to repeat, again and again and again. You will think you have "got" it, but still the instructor will ask you to keep practicing. Subtle changes occur as you continue to practice; gradually, if you pay attention, you will understand the movements differently, and from that inner understanding will develop power and speed. It takes time, patience, and perseverance. An old Chinese saying counsels, "Do the movement a thousand times, it will become natural." When it's natural, it's truly yours—a correct habit that can be produced instinctively under great pressure at any time.

There is no substitute for repetition; it is the only road to mastery.

Advice

The following advice is offered to help you benefit the most from every workout session.

First, arrive on time and plan to stay until the end of the session. Arriving late or leaving early will disturb the class and shortchange you in your training. If you need to change clothes before class, arrive in plenty of time to do that and settle down, in order to be both mentally and physically ready when the session begins.

Second, give your full attention. During demonstrations, do not talk or chat or whisper; this shows disrespect to the teacher, disturbs others, and compromises your own learning.

Allow your body to learn without the interference of your mind. Relax. Focus totally on observing. This is particularly true if the Chief Instructor is demonstrating, because his or her form will probably be the best available to you to learn from. As the Chief Instructor demonstrates, at first do not analyze, do not even try to mimic the movements (unless the class has been asked to follow along); instead simply *watch*. It has been shown that the body learns best without interference from thinking. Therefore, quiet your mind, focus your attention, be aware that every joint, muscle, tendon, and bone are involved in the proper execution of the form, and then simply absorb what you see. What you will be watching will be beyond the mind's analytical comprehension; that is, any complex movement—such as a kung fu form—requires such subtle coordination of such a range of muscles with a sequence, rhythm, and timing that the mind cannot possibly grasp it all. Do not try. Allow your body to learn.

If you have trouble remembering the sequence of movements in a form, don't worry. Worry will make your memory even worse. Keep practicing; eventually you will get it.

Then, throughout this and every subsequent workout session, watch the sifu and senior instructors as often as possible. When the sifu is demonstrating something to someone else in the class, even in a different part of the room, students will often stop what they are doing in order to go watch. Kung fu is a performing art, and you simply need to watch it to learn how to do it.

After demonstrating the form, the instructor is likely to explain how to do it—what to avoid doing, what to be sure to do, how to do it most easily. Sometimes instructors will also explain fighting applications, and demonstrate these with a partner. Usually students do not ask questions during the demonstrations; usually the instructor has a plan for explaining and introducing new material, and you should let him or her finish. This is polite not only toward the instructor but also toward other students. Usually at the end of his demonstration/presentation, the instructor will ask for questions. At that time, if any-

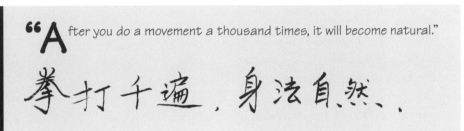

"After you do a movement a thousand times, it will become natural."

拳打千遍，身法自然。

thing is still unclear, that is the time to ask. But don't press any point; if you are having serious problems—and this is likely, especially at the beginning of your training—then wait until later and ask for personal help from an assistant instructor. This will be best for you and the rest of the class.

Take full advantage of small group workouts. Often, after the demonstration the class will break up into small groups of two, three, or four people for work on new and/or previously learned material. This has several benefits. First, it puts people of differing experience and understanding together; the less experienced can learn from the more advanced. Second, it will help you all remember everything. As the old saying goes, "two heads are better than one"—with others you will be able to piece together all that the instructor has said and demonstrated. Third, working through the new material among your peers will probably be more comfortable for you as you gain confidence in the movements. Finally, practicing together in a group or with a partner will give you the chance to try out the applications, to see how a block or a punch or a kick at a particular point in the form actually works. This will greatly improve your form, as your body will understand the movement in the context of a real situation, rather than simply as a gymnastic exercise.

Do not compare yourself with others with regard to speed of learning or skill. People differ in how they learn and how fast they learn. Some people need a lot of time practicing alone, repeating the forms over and over until they have understood and memorized them; others learn quickly and are able to repeat the forms after only one or two demonstrations. You may find that you learn some kinds of movements very quickly, while you just can't seem to catch on to others. Do not let this worry you. Neither be discouraged by slow progress, nor impatient and arrogant if you are learning quickly. In fact, learning slowly can be an advantage in the long run. Experienced sifus know that sometimes quick learners do not learn thoroughly. They catch on so fast that they feel they have mastered a movement before they have repeated it enough to really understand it. They are eager and seem ready to move on, but they are in danger of forgetting what they just learned as quickly as they picked it up. In contrast, slow learners are more likely to develop a solid foundation for a good practice in the long run because they may have to repeat the movement hundreds of times in order to remember it. They don't have confidence, so they keep practicing, and that practicing builds muscle memory as well as skill. If you learn more slowly than others, accept the fact that you will not be able to perform any new movement perfectly the first time, nor even the second or third time. Eventually, however, with perseverance you will achieve your goal—and your form will show the hours of hard work and effort you have put into it. If you learn fast, take care; look for details that might be escaping you.

Be patient; learning slowly can mean learning more thoroughly.

Similarly, with regard to skill, don't be critical of yourself or of others; there are many reasons why one person may be faster, stronger, smoother, more graceful—or less so—than others. Even more important, you may not know how to judge kung fu, especially at the beginning stages. What seems dramatic and awesome may have no inner power. Critical comparison and judgment serve no useful purpose. Rather than wasting time in comparison, your best strategy is to listen to your instructor's advice, watch, and work continuously, with determination and diligence.

Do not be shy about practicing or performing in front of the instructors. Their role is to teach you good kung fu, but they can correct your mistakes only if they see them. They do not expect you to "get" it immediately. You can be sure that, no matter how good or bad you are, they have probably seen better

Avoid any thoughts of judgment or criticism, of yourself or others.

and worse. You must practice in order to learn. The more you practice correctly, the more quickly you will advance. So, practice hard while you are at the school so that the instructors can be sure your stances, punches, and footwork have the correct basic form before you leave.

When you practice, give your all. When you feel your energy flagging and need to take a break, step off quietly to the side and rest. When you begin to feel tired, you will not learn effectively and your movements will start to be sloppy. This is counterproductive. A few minutes' rest and a drink should refresh you for another round of practice.

The final piece of advice is to enjoy yourself. Practice with dedication, but also with enthusiasm and pleasure. Participating in workout sessions is the core of your kung fu training and will bring many immeasurable rewards.

chapter 14
drills and
conditioning exercises

DRILLS AND CONDITIONING EXERCISES are an essential, albeit less glamorous, aspect of kung fu training. As in any other art or sport, repetitive drills are necessary to build the muscles and skills to perform or execute the art. One cannot exist without the other. Most styles of kung fu have their own traditional exercises, specific to the particular stances, punches, and/or kicks that characterize their forms, and these will not be covered here. Instead, what will be covered are the general principles and goals of conditioning and some of the exercises that are common to a wide variety of kung fu styles. Much of this aspect of training is left to the individual, both as to what you do and how much time you spend at it. Once you begin training, you will get a sense of what your weak points are and where you need strengthening. You may also ask your instructor for an assessment and for advice as to how to improve.

This phrase expresses the importance of including drills in your kung fu training:

"If you practice movements (forms) but not drills, your life may be long but empty."

練拳不練功, 到老一場空.

Why Drill?

In general, drills are devised to develop these five important attributes.

Speed

In fighting situations speed is considered more important than technique. It comes from flexibility and looseness: a relaxed, limber muscle, directed by pure intention, can move with lightning swiftness. Thus, developing speed has several components: first, improving concentration; second, relaxing muscles when they are not needed; and finally, moving limbs (arms, legs) smoothly. You may develop speed in any movement by practicing it repetitively, patiently, and with focus. The more you do it, the easier it should become, and as it becomes easier, it should become faster. Just be sure you maintain proper form at all times, and don't take shortcuts that may seem to make it easier, but will compromise the effectiveness of the movement in the long run.

Power

Power has two components. One component is the sheer strength of muscles and tendons; the second is the ability to deliver the full amount of that strength to the target. To build muscles, weight lifting, push-ups, dynamic tension exercises, isometric exercises, and the like—any and all will serve the purpose. Delivering the power depends on relaxed and flexible muscles. (This concept is described in more detail in Chapter 11, "Hand Techniques." Training this aspect is a matter of concentration and understanding developed through the experience of repetitive drills of virtually any movement.

Endurance

It is said that endurance is the most difficult of all the physical attributes to develop, possibly because it is the physical counterpart of the mental attributes needed to develop it—patience and perseverance. For Chinese martial artists, the horse stance is the classic exercise used to develop endurance. This is because the strength of the legs is the reservoir of the body's energy; using the legs develops endurance, especially in slow and/or repetitive exercises in which the legs bear the body weight. Thus, any exercise that uses the legs in this way will develop endurance: jumping rope, jogging, kicking exercises, hopping, and others.

Flexibility

To develop flexibility, the main strategy is to perform specific stretching exercises regularly, thus opening the joints, and then to use the joints repetitively, thus developing the muscles to support them.

Balance

Practice any movements or stances in which you feel unsteady. Devise your own exercises to improve your balance. One of the best exercises to train balance is to assume the crane stance and hold the raised foot with the opposite hand. Hold the stance for as long as you can, and repeat on both sides (See Chapter 12, "Warming Up").

How to Drill

Broadly speaking, drills are of two types: One consists of drills specifically created as such; you may know some of these, or your instructor will teach them to you. The second consists of drills that come from a form. That is, you may simply take a few movements from any form and repeat them continuously, concentrating on whatever attribute seems weakest, be it smoothness, speed, or agility.

Conditioning Exercises

The following describe some of the more common and universally adopted exercises, familiar to students of a wide range of kung fu styles and particularly designed to develop the muscles needed for kung fu forms.

Push-ups

There is probably no better exercise, East or West, for developing arm strength than the push-up. In kung fu training the push-up is a sequential training that strengthens not only the shoulders and elbows, but also the wrists and fingers. As in the Western style, your body should be held flat, supported only by your toes, with your knees straight. Your hands should be placed on the ground under your shoulders. At the first level, place your palms flat on the ground. At the second level, use your fists instead of your palms; keep your wrists straight and thumbs tucked out of the way, just as you would do for the proper punching fist. At the third level, extend your fingers and support your body on the five fingertips; at the next level, use only three fingers (thumb, index fin-

Figure 14-1: Push-ups

ger, and middle finger); then only two fingers (thumb, index finger). And, finally, support the body and execute the push-up using only the thumbs for support. For even further exercise, you can put a weight (a sandbag or books, for example) on your back and then do the push-ups.

How many to do? Begin with what you can manage, and gradually increase. You should probably be able to do twenty to fifty at any level before proceeding to the next level.

Horse Stance

The horse stance is a popular and extremely effective exercise for developing leg strength, balance, endurance, and the solidity necessary for executing effective punches and kicks. Your legs and feet should be positioned as described in Chapter 8, "Stances." Your arms can be held in any of a number of positions, depending on what you are trying to accomplish or which part of your arms you are trying to strengthen. The most common form, perhaps, is to hold the fists at the waist, arms bent and elbows extending back; this expands the chest. Another simple formation is to stretch the arms directly out to the sides, holding them flat at shoulder level with fingers also flat and extended. Yet another position is to hold the arms in a circle in front of the body. For hard training sink the stance until your thighs are nearly parallel to the ground, and hold your hands with the backs facing your chest (palms facing outward). For more gentle (internal) training, assume a more narrow and relaxed horse stance (that is, with your legs a little wider than shoulders' width), and hold your arms in a relaxed circle with the palms facing inward, as though holding a big ball in front of your chest. In both cases, your arms should make a smooth and graceful circle, and your shoulders should be relaxed, allowing your head to sit freely on top of your neck.

The height of the horse stance determines the degree of training.

There are other variations; the main point is to relax your upper body while your lower body sinks, developing a feeling of lightness above and a sense of solidity or heaviness below. The deeper you sink, the more vigorous the training.

How long to hold the position? The longer the better. Begin with whatever you can manage, and gradually increase to whatever time you can tolerate. In the past students were asked to hold the horse stance for hours; today ten to twenty minutes is probably a good goal for general benefit and regular training.

Punching Bag

For conditioning fists and arms, the classic punching bag used in kung fu training was a canvas bag filled with rice. Today any ordinary punching bag will serve the same purpose. Such bags are usually suspended from the ceiling. To use one, assume a horse stance or front stance facing the bag, and then punch. You may practice all fist and punching techniques, including willow leaf palm, on such a bag. Be sure to practice both sides equally.

There are at least three benefits from this practice. First, it conditions the hands and arms. The impact of repeated punching toughens the skin and strengthens the bones. Second, it strengthens all the muscles involved in hand techniques (palm, fist, forearm, elbow, and the rest) from legs to waist to arm to forearm. Third, it teaches the rhythm and coordination required to deliver the power of the entire body through the hand. This is especially critical in performing the forms because in the forms, your oppo-

Benefits of Punching Bag Practice

1. Toughens skin

2. Strengthens bones and muscles

3. Teaches rhythm and coordinationw

nent is imaginary. Working with the punching bag will show you what it's like to hit a real object (or body) so that later, in executing a form, you will have the physical sense of it and be able to reproduce the subtle sequence of movements that will make it appear that you are having a real fight in the form.

There is no fixed period for using the punching bag. Naturally, the longer, the more often, and the more regularly you work with it, the better the results. Ideally, after finishing a workout, you should go directly to the bag, as your muscles will be thoroughly warmed and your joints loosened, and the proper forms of the movements will be fresh in your mind (and in your body!). Go easy at the beginning; do not punch so hard that you bruise your knuckles or damage your hand. That is counterproductive. Slow and steady wins the race: start slowly and gently with what you can comfortably manage, then try to strike a little harder, a little more often, a little faster every day—always maintaining correct form.

Figure 14-2: Iron palm training

Iron Palm

The purpose of iron palm training is to toughen and condition the hand. This is a specialized conditioning, not required or even expected of every student; nevertheless, it is one of the traditional kung fu conditioning exercises, and probably used in every style, so we include it here for information. For those who want to attempt it, it will be best to ask for an instructor's help and guidance.

For iron palm training, you need a bag filled with sand or BBs. These bags may be available in your school; they may also be bought at martial arts supply stores, or you can make one yourself. To make your own, you will need fine-textured, heavy material, such as canvas or denim, and strong thread for sewing. Decide on the size according to the size of your hand; nine inches by nine inches is a good average size. You will need at least two bags: fill one with fine sand for the first stage of

The traditional term for iron palm training is "practicing the hand." As expressed in the phrase above, in traditional training "hand practice" typically came at the end of the workout, when the body was well warmed.

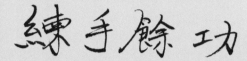

training, and fill a second with BB shot for the later stage.

While the concept and purpose of the iron palm bag are the same for all styles of kung fu, the specifics of how the bag is oriented and how the bag is used differ; your instructor should be able to teach you the method of the style followed in your school. That is, sometimes the bag is placed on a table; for other types of training it may be hung up. In some styles, only the heel and back of the hand are conditioned, while in others, the outside edge of the hand and the finger tips are also conditioned. In some styles, one hand is conditioned (front, back, edge, fingertips) repetitively and then the other; in other styles, hands strike the bag alternately and repetitively. The time spent in iron palm training also differs; generally it is recommended to practice every day for a period of ten to thirty minutes. Again, your instructor should teach you the details.

The Chinese liniment *dit da jow* can prevent injury if rubbed into the hand before training.

For one common usage, place the bag at about waist height. Assume a solid stance (for example, either the horse stance or front stance) facing the bag. Strike the bag with the heel of one hand and then the other. Raise your arm, and let it fall, striking the bag soundly—first one arm and then the other, in an even, comfortable rhythm. Concentrate, but don't try to use too much power—especially before your hand is conditioned—or you could damage your hand. Begin slowly, strive for a smooth, even rhythm, and gradually build strength.

If you are training seriously, then an important prerequisite is the use of the traditional Chinese liniment dit da jow ("fall and strike wine"), which should be rubbed into the hand before each session of training. (See Chapter

17, "Safety," for details.) Dit da jow will help conditioning by preventing bruises in the short term and chronic injury in the long term.

Piercing Hand

For those styles that incorporate the piercing hand, the traditional exercise for training this technique involves thrusting the hand into buckets filled with materials of gradually increasing roughness. Again, as with iron palm training, this is neither required nor expected of every student, but it is a traditional conditioning exercise known to most styles. At the first stage, the bucket is filled with rice. The practitioner forms the piercing hand (see Chapter 11, "Hand techniques") and thrusts the four fingers into the bucket up to the knuckles. After he or she is accustomed to this, at the next level, the bucket is filled with beans, then fine sand, and finally small pieces of gravel.

There is no fixed period for this practice; the extent and intensity depend on what you are trying to accomplish. Rely on your instructor for details and guidance.

Figure 14-3: Piercing hand

Finger Weight Lifting

In many of the styles, claws and claw hands are important parts of the techniques—tiger claw, eagle claw, and the like (see Chapter 11). To develop the necessary strength in the fingers, especially at the small joints, the technique is to lift weighted jars by gripping the lids with your fingers. (Note: This exercise also develops arm and back muscles.) The jars should be of a diameter to fit your hand comfortably, so that your fingers fit around the rim in about the same pattern as when you make the claw. Plastic is safer than glass because if you drop it, it won't crack or break. Ideally, you should use two jars of exactly the same size and weight, and train both hands/arms simultaneously. Fill the jars with anything heavy—sand, for example. Grip the jars by their lids, assume a

Figure 14-4: Finger weight lifting (jar lift)

horse stance, then slowly, deliberately lift the jars to shoulder height; pause, then slowly lower the jars. Try to keep your arms more or less straight, but don't lock your elbows. Repeat. Start with less weight, and gradually increase; avoid lifting one jar at a time, especially when they are very heavy, because the unbalanced strain can pull a muscle in your back.

Wooden Dummy

At later stages of study and practice, kung fu students will be introduced to the wooden dummy. This is a stout wooden post, of the diameter of a medium-sized tree, with wooden beams or "arms" jutting out at various heights and angles. It is a common fixture in most kung fu schools and used by most students, eventually, in their training.

To use it, one "attacks" the various arms with different hand, arm, and leg techniques. There are particular forms for using the dummies (as with other forms). Using the wooden dummy conditions both arms and legs and teaches timing and coordination, while giving more of a sense of real combat.

Figure 14-5: Wooden dummy

forms

FORMS ARE A TRADITIONAL MEANS of teaching kung fu. Each form, like a dance, is a set sequence of movements, but in this case the movements are martial arts techniques—punches, blocks, kicks, and the rest—and they are organized to represent a fight. Each style of kung fu has its own set of forms that have been created over centuries and handed down from generation to generation through demonstration and practice. After learning the basic elements of a particular style, beginners will quickly progress to learning forms, and from then on, most of the rest of their training will be learning different forms.

Because forms will be such an important part of your kung fu life, knowing something of how they were created and why they are useful, as well as how to learn them, should be helpful.

Origins

Where do the forms of a particular style come from? Traditionally, forms were created by masters for their students for purposes of training or exercise or for teaching fighting strategy. Thus, in any given kung fu style, the repertory of forms is a collection of both those forms passed down from previous generations and those forms created by living masters. In most cases, the purpose or guiding principle in the creation of forms was to help students learn and develop faster, better, more effectively. In that sense, the original motivation behind a given form could have been very specific, based on an individual sifu's experience and observation of particular students. Sifus may have seen certain recurring problems in their students and created the forms to help them overcome those particular problems. Masters also created forms to represent their particular fighting strategy. Through experience, they may have found that certain combinations of movements or certain techniques were particularly effective and thus, they attempted to preserve and pass down this wisdom in a form.

Historically, forms served purposes of exercise, education, reference, and performance.

In addition, during the Ching dynasty (1644–1911), forms were created for performance. During this period, the Manchurians sought to eliminate potential rebels and particularly targeted martial artists, forbidding the local Han people from carrying weapons or practicing martial arts. To hide their identity, many fighters earned their living as part of opera troupes and as street performers, and stories were created with many battles and fight scenes. Thus, they were able to practice their art in public, but this also meant that forms were created with many flashy, acrobatic movements to disguise serious practice as dancing and to please audiences.

Today forms are also created specifically for competition—in wushu, the modern Chinese version or interpretation of kung fu (see Part 1: "Introduction"). Wushu forms are created both for international competitions and for major celebrations in China. The purposes of these forms are to challenge performers with the complete range of technique and to ensure that the winner of the competition will truly demonstrate mastery of the art. By creating a new form for each competition, the Wushu Committee also ensures that all competitors have equal time for practice. In this case, mastery of the form is meant to demonstrate expertise, skill, and grace, but not necessarily readiness for combat, as in the case of traditional kung fu.

Names

Each form has a name. Many of the older, traditional forms have poetic or figurative names, invoking images from nature (for example, Mantis Exits the Cave, Single-Thrust Blossom, Tiger Crane); others are named after their creator or after the place where they were first devised (such as Dragon Lake Leg, Hung Family Form). Similarly, the movements that make up the traditional

In the past, poetic names were used to keep techniques secret, within the family. Today they have been abandoned in favor of descriptive terms.

forms also have poetic names (Black Dragon Swinging Tail, Single-Leg Hungry Crane, Zig-Zag Butterfly Palm). These names served several purposes. First, being unique and colorful, they were memorable. Second, they gave some hint as to the inner aspects of the techniques and helped practitioners understand how to execute them properly. Invoking images from nature especially helped with this, by recalling the natural, smooth, and effective characteristics of animal movement. Finally, and perhaps most important in those early days, the poetic names served as a kind of code that kept rival schools and styles from learning the secret techniques of another school. While you and your fellow students would know immediately what the "Continuous Fire Arrow" was, it would be a mystery to outsiders.

In the twentieth century, the poetic names of the movements have mostly been replaced with descriptive terms—right forward punch, upper block, down strike, and so on. In contrast to yesteryear, today the way to ensure that the techniques will be preserved accurately is clear and efficient communication among many, rather than secrecy among a selected few.

Functions

The forms serve important functions, both for the art and for the artists:

1. First, in terms of the art, the forms have served as a kind of *encyclopedia or reference manual* of the techniques of any given style. In the past (before video recordings), maintaining the purity and accuracy of the techniques from generation to generation was as problematical as it was critical. Students practiced diligently to perform the forms accurately throughout their training career, knowing that their execution of the techniques was the only way the next generation could learn. Just as a sentence is easier to remember than a list of words, techniques that were linked in a meaningful sequence—the form—were (and are) easier to recall. Thus, the forms functioned as the best available means to maintain the style and pass down the techniques from generation to generation.

2. For students, then, the forms were the fundamental reference materials of their study. In addition—and for the same reasons that made them

good as references—forms were and are the *basic learning materials*. Techniques are simply easier, if not more fun, to learn when strung together in a sequence. The flow helps the body make sense of the movements; the sequence helps ensure that no technique is overlooked. At the same time, forms make teaching easier. In most styles forms can be

> A form is like a sentence, composed of different movements rather than words. Just as it's easier to remember a sentence than a list of words, so it has always been easier for students to memorize techniques by learning forms.

grouped according to level of difficulty, so there are certain forms that are typically taught first and those that are typically reserved for advanced students. In a sense, the lesson plan is fixed. Thus, forms are convenient and effective educational tools for both learners and instructors.

3. Most important for the student, perhaps, *forms train the body*; practicing them improves endurance, balance, and coordination—all of which are critical attributes when it comes to a real fight. Having to perform the techniques in different sequences (that is, in different forms) means that students must learn each technique thoroughly; they must be able to execute each one no matter what comes before it and no matter what comes after. This requires good flexibility, coordination, and timing; it teaches the transfer, flow, and optimal use of power.

4. Forms also *train the mind*. To perform the form correctly, you must remember the sequence. In the beginning this requires that your full attention be focused on the physical performance of the form: getting the order correct and performing each movement accurately. After many repetitions, the sequence becomes automatic, and your mind can then consider the meaning of the form as an enactment of an actual fight. Then, you will go on to learn another form. . . . So, in practicing, you must keep your mind alert and aware of which form you are doing and which technique comes next. Again, this maintains mental acuity (and keeps one from getting bored, as can happen doing repetitive drills).

5. As *representations of real fights*, forms provide important physical and mental training in continuous, focused effort. A fight is a sequence— your opponent punches, you block; you kick, your opponent blocks; and so on—so you need to be familiar and comfortable with shifting from one movement/technique to another. A fight is nonstop, so you need endur-

ance. A fight is spontaneous and unpredictable, so you need to learn different forms to train different sequences—especially forms from different masters, representing different fighting strategies. *And* your mind must be alert. While forms help train all of these attributes, of course no real fight will occur as the forms portray. Not only will the sequence differ, but also, in a real fight many of the aspects of the aggressor will be unpredictable—your opponent could be large, small, agile or clumsy, powerful or weak, righthanded or lefthanded, and so forth. You will have to adjust your technique and strategy instantly and spontaneously. The different forms—different combinations, different sequences, sometimes different techniques—all represent different strategies. If you remain alert, experience in executing the different techniques in different combinations, and using other people's philosophies and strategies will prepare you to develop your own fighting style—and to fight effectively when needed.

Forms train endurance, coordination, and flexibility.

6. Forms also offer *opportunity for individuality*. Here enters the artistic aspects of kung fu. Although the sequence is fixed, although the basic movements of the techniques are prescribed, the actual execution by any individual will be just that—individual. In the flow of the movements, people can express their individuality. Watching beginners, even at the early stages, one can see the individual differences in timing and coordination, as well as the execution of individual movements. This is the seed of the beauty and personal expression of power that will develop with training, and these are the elements that have attracted and fascinated audiences since the early days of martial arts displays.

7. Finally, today forms are also the means for *evaluating achievement and demonstrating skill*. Public demonstrations often consist of forms, and they are events for competition at tournaments. As beginners develop greater strength and ability, the instructor will assign forms of increasing difficulty to challenge and develop their skill even further. All those

familiar with a particular school or style will be able to judge students' progress and ability by which forms they know and by how well they perform certain forms. Indeed, in some martial arts styles, certain specific forms

> **F**orms are progressive: the students' progress can be gauged by the forms that they do, as well as by how skillfully they do them.

are used as benchmarks for progress and achievement. When the instructor decides to teach a more advanced style, the student knows that he or she has achieved a certain level of skill. At the same time, any form can reveal a student's level by the way it is performed. The beginning student will be able to demonstrate accuracy, while advanced students will show subtler and deeper understanding of the movements. Just as in music, although a student of any level may be able to play Beethoven, the beginning student will show mastery of the notes, while the advanced student will use the notes expressively.

Learning Forms

Forms are of different lengths and levels of difficulty. In most styles, the sequence in which the forms are taught/learned is more or less standard, having been fixed through generations of teaching. Beginners start with shorter, less complex forms, and gradually move on to longer, more challenging forms. Even so, just as in other arts, such as music and dance, advanced students also find it a challenge to perform the simple forms with more depth as their skill progresses and their understanding deepens.

In general, the instructor will decide which forms a student will learn. Only experienced students may ask to be taught a specific form.

The beginner can expect to begin learning forms very early in the training process, although, of course, this will differ according to the style, the school, and the sifu, as well as the student's ability. At first, the student will be taught simple forms comprising fewer movements and less complex techniques. At this stage the student will not only be learning the individual movements, but also gaining familiarity with their names (horse stance, upper cut, replacing punch, thrust kick, and the rest). Learning the names is actually more important than it may seem at the time, and full attention should be paid to associating these names with the movement. Learning these names will make learning more complex forms much easier, as you will already have an automatic mental label for the movements that must be remembered. Also, when instructors correct you, you'll know what they are talking about; for them, the names of the movements and forms have become second nature, so they will probably try to help you and correct you by calling out the movement names. When you can understand and respond instantly, all will go more smoothly.

In tackling a new form, here are some guidelines as to how to proceed:

1. **Memorize it**. The first step is to memorize the sequence of movements. Simply learn how to do it. You should be able to go from start to finish without pause. Keep practicing until the sequence is automatic.

2. **Perfect balance and alignment; become aware of coordination and timing**. Once you know the sequence, try to improve your balance and alignment. You should be firm on your feet at all times, whether weight is evenly distributed or not. You should feel and look solid, with appropriate alignment of head, spine, and lower body. If there are mirrors, use them to correct your posture. Pause often in the form to check—is your spine straight? Are your shoulders relaxed? Feet properly placed for the stance? Begin to be aware of how your hands and feet move relative to each other. Which moves first? Or are they simultaneous? The timing and coordination are partly a result of the applications, which will be your focus in the next stage.

3. **Learn the applications**. Having memorized the form, steadied your stances, and corrected the alignment of your body and limbs, you must next understand the meaning of the movements in terms of an imaginary opponent. This meaning is called the "applications." Understanding the applications will allow you to correct the timing and coordination of your hands and feet, and you will be able to make the movements more intelligent—that is, perform them as though you were actually hitting or striking or blocking. This will give your form meaning, as well as grace and power.

   Usually the instructor will demonstrate the applications of each movement of the form with another instructor or student. Pay particular attention to the coordination of hands and feet. Which moves first? Or do they move at the same time? In general, the feet move before the hands/arms, as expressed in a traditional martial arts saying: "If the feet arrive, but the hands do not, you can't hit the opponent. If the hands arrive before the feet, hitting the person is like beating grass." Just about the only way you can learn this timing and coordination is from watching. You must pay careful attention to develop a physical understanding of how the movements should feel and flow as you execute the form.

After the demonstration, find a partner, and practice yourself. Get the feeling of what a "block" or "elbow strike" or "kidney strike" actually feels

> **66** If the feet arrive but the hands do not, you can't hit the opponent. If the hands arrive before the feet, punching is like beating grass."
>
> 步到手不到，打人打不倒．
>
> 手到步不到，打人如把草．

like when you do it to someone else and what it feels like to receive such a strike or block. Once you can visualize the movements of the form as responses to what the opponent is doing—blocking a strike, punching to an exposed region, moving forward to execute an attack or backward to avoid one—coordination and timing should come more naturally, and you will add an extra dimension of meaning to what you are doing.

4. **Smooth out the transitions**. Next, concentrate on smoothness. Having learned the individual movements thoroughly and precisely, having understood their purpose and coordinated them, now try to connect the movements with fluidity and grace so that the entire form flows from beginning to end. In smoothness there is economy of motion and energy. When one motion naturally connects with the next, movements support each other, and maximum power can be delivered in the applications. At the same time, do not forget earlier lessons: Remain solidly rooted to the ground and stable at all times. Do not rush movements or cut them short; finish each one before starting the next. Remember the proper coordination of hands and feet. But now aim to connect the movements

in a fluid sequence. Make that space between movements less distinct. To teach the form, it had to be broken down into steps; now erase those artificial divisions and make the form appear continuous.

As you become more proficient, take care that you do not become sloppy. Never rush movements; finish each one before starting the next.

5. **Develop power and speed**. Finally—when you have mastered all the previous steps, and not before—turn your attention to power and speed. When you can execute the form precisely, automatically, and smoothly, you will also be able to do it quickly with little effort. Remaining aware of the applications, focus your attention and intention to deliver power through the movements as intended.

> **"T**he feet are the roots; the legs are the source of power; the waist is the director [determining how, when, and where the power of the legs is used]. Ultimately, the power arrives at and is expressed through the fingertips."

其根在腳，發於腿．主宰於腰，形於手指．

In classical Chinese, the distribution of power is described as follows: "The feet are the roots; the legs are the source of power; the waist is the director or judge that determines how, when, and where the power of the legs is used. Ultimately, the power arrives at the fingertips."

Furthermore, the concentration and focus of power is said to derive from the "Six Harmonies and Three Sections." The Six Harmonies are the harmonies of corresponding joints, namely: wrists and ankles; knees and elbows; shoulders and hips. The Three Sections refer to the three joints that control the flow of power in the upper and lower regions of the body, as follows: Power from the shoulder flows through the elbow and is emitted through the fist, while power from the hip flows through the knee and is expressed in the foot. With the feet providing a solid foundation and control maintained by the waist, proper alignment ensures delivery of full power to the target.

While this is considered advanced theory, the beginner can perhaps benefit from glimpsing what is ahead. Understanding body structure and dynamics is also part of the training.

Practice!

Having said all that, the only message left is to repeat and emphasize the importance of PRACTICE at every step along the way. Review and repeat. When you think you'll never get it, continue to practice. Review and repeat. Improvement is cyclical, not linear. When you think you know it so well that you couldn't possibly improve, continue to practice. Review and repeat. More practice will bring more familiarity, more sensitivity, and more awareness. Success is ensured.

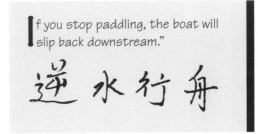

If you stop paddling, the boat will slip back downstream."

逆 水 行 舟

internal training

MENTAL TRAINING in kung fu has three aspects, roughly following the three philosophical roots of Taoism, Buddhism, and Confucianism. These aspects are: learning to enhance and guide internal energy (qi); disciplining the mind and emotions; and developing virtue.

Qi

The concept of internal energy, or vital essence, goes back thousands of years in both Western and Eastern cultures. The Greeks called it "fire"; the Chinese call it qi. Qi was a central concept in the Zen Buddhism taught by Bodhidharma at the Shaolin Temple and is compatible with concepts of the Tao as espoused by Lao-tzu. The idea is that each person, as part of the universe, has access to the universal energy that animates the natural world. The anatomical region below the navel—called the dan tian—is the body's reservoir of qi. You can learn to absorb energy from the natural world, store it in your dan tian, and then use it at will. This is primarily a process of mental training. By using your mind to focus on various body parts, you can coordinate and enhance your inner energy and physical power. Certain exercises have been devised specifically to increase qi, clear blockages in the paths through which it flows (the "meridians," in classical Chinese medical theory), and develop smooth, strong flow of qi throughout the body. This flow has the power not only to build fighting strength, but also to cure disease, strengthen the immune system, and generally promote health. Many of the extraordinary feats of the Shaolin Temple martial artists—and of martial artists today—derive from control of the qi. Thus, developing qi is essential to achievement in kung fu, but this is introduced only later at advanced levels, and its teaching is best left to personal instruction. Hence, no more will be said here.

his phrase expresses the essence of how the Chinese understand energy transformation in the body:

"Physical Energy (Jing) melts into Vital Energy (Qi); Vital Energy melts into Spirit (Shen). Shen follows the Tao [the unlimited source of cosmic energy]."

鍊精化氣, 鍊氣化神, 鍊神還虛.

Mind Control

A second aspect of internal training has to do with disciplining the mind and controlling the emotions. The purpose is to give you the power to accomplish what you set out to do: that is, to set a goal, and then to focus all of your efforts on achieving that goal. It is the power to keep your mind clear of distractions, and then, with that clear mind, to act spontaneously, immediately, and appropriately as you need to. This sort of power is valuable in virtually every sphere of your life.

Once you acknowledge the value of disciplining your mind, the main means of accomplishing it is—simply—to do it. There are two broad approaches: One is practiced when the body is active; the other is practiced when the body is still (commonly called "meditation").

When the Body Is Active

When your body is active, such as during training sessions or at any time in your daily life, you can practice mental discipline. The technique is straight-forward: Just concentrate exclusively on what you are doing. No matter what

Disciplining the mind can be done at any time—whether the body is in motion or at rest.

it is, whether walking the dog or executing a thrust kick, give it your full attention, notice every detail about the process, banish any thought that is not relevant to the task at hand. This develops your power of concentration and brings calmness.

When the Body Is Still

You may also practice mental discipline when your body is inactive—typically in special sessions called meditations. Meditation takes many forms, and each school—each meditator—will have his or her own preference. Sometimes teachers ask that meditators assume particular postures; sitting cross-legged with hands in the lap is common. In kung fu training the horse stance can be used for this purpose, as it can train the body at the same time. Sometimes teachers may ask meditators to focus their attention—for example, on the breath as it enters and leaves the nostrils or on the diaphragm or dan tian; other teachers may ask meditators to empty their minds.

In both cases—whether the body is active or still—your task is the same: When you notice that your mind has wandered, simply bring it back to awareness of the task at hand. Do not waste effort blaming yourself or feeling failure—that is not helping the task at hand! Instead, simply settle down to focusing on the present with even more determination. That is practicing and developing discipline—sticking to the preset goal. By repeatedly doing this, you will develop a strong mind and strong concentration.

Eventually, too, when you are able to concentrate, you may notice that your mind feels "empty." According to Chinese medical theory and observation, when the mind is empty, the qi automatically circulates, restoring vitality to the cells and rejuvenating tissues. This belief now has support from experimental evidence. In meditation, as breathing becomes slower, deeper, and

Resting the mind rejuvenates the body.

more even, tissues and organs relax; oxygen-rich blood reaches more cells; hormones induce relaxation and relieve stress. For the martial artist, this means not only increased vitality, but also increased endurance and power.

Indeed, at the point of pure concentration and focus, the mind *is* empty: empty of emotion and ego, as well as empty of distractions. In that pure space is the ability to react spontaneously, wholeheartedly, and with full power to whatever need arises. That ability may also be described as sensitivity. You learn to see, to feel, and to experience the present moment and all that is happening in it more clearly. In fights you can sense what your opponents are going to do before they do it—and then initiate effective countermeasures.

Developing Virtue

The third aspect of internal training that is integral to the martial arts is developing virtue. This is accomplished through meditation, through study of the scriptures (Buddhist, Taoist, and Confucian classics), through personal instruc-

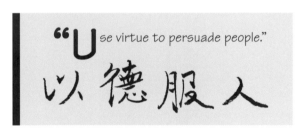
"Use virtue to persuade people."
以 德 服 人

tion from sifus, and simply from association with persons of integrity. Through these means, one gains wisdom; one learns a sense of responsibility and respect; and one naturally develops compassion. A fundamental tenet of Buddhism maintains that each person has—or is—the seed of a living Buddha. Meditation gradually reveals this seed, gradually bringing out one's finest qualities and true nature.

Such qualities have direct influence on one's martial arts training and ability. Gradually, one overcomes ego and the emotions that arise as a result of ego, such as anger, hate, feelings of revenge, and arrogance. Eventually, one understands that the best use of power is to avoid conflict: "The good sword never leaves its scabbard."

Mind-Qi-Strength

In kung fu understanding the relationship between intention (mind), internal energy (qi), and physical strength is critical to developing effective fighting technique. It is said, "Physical force has an end, but the mind/intention has no end." Any physical motion—in this case, a punch, block, or kick, for example—has a beginning and end, but not the mind/intention. Mind is continuous. To win a fight, the mind must have the firm intention to win. As soon as one technique is executed, even before it is finished, the mind must be preparing the next—either ready to block or ready to execute another offensive maneuver. The mind/intention must be totally focused on the opponent, and what he or she is preparing to do: in that way, defense becomes as continuous as intention.

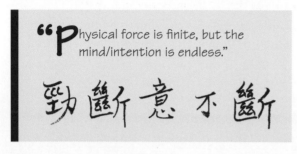

"**P**hysical force is finite, but the mind/intention is endless."

A second phrase captures the flow of action: "As soon as intention/mind moves, qi is there; when qi arrives, strength is immediately expressed." From this, two things are clear: Effective action depends on clear intention. Qi is an integral link in the full expression of physical strength. Clearly, then, mental training is fundamental in the development of a martial artist.

Progress in Training: What to Look For

As your training progresses, you may notice changes in your strength and flexibility, but that is probably not all that is happening. Usually, you will also be experiencing important progress in mental development, which is absolutely critical to your overall training and inseparable from your physical development. For example, in the first stage of training, you learn technique—the external forms. Observe your mind. You may think you are doing well at the

"**A**s soon as mind/intention moves, qi moves; when qi arrives, there is immediate physical expression."

意之所到. 氣之所達. 氣之所達. 力即箸焉.

beginning, but as your skill improves, you discover your movements are in fact sloppy, so you improve. You begin to understand balance, coordination, rhythm, and timing at a deeper level; you become more sensitive. Through that sensitivity, you can really improve. Similarly, as your sensitivity to your physical movements increases, so you become more sensitive to your attitudes and behavior. Once you let go of ego, then respect and humility automatically step in. Once you become aware of the consequences of pride and dishonesty, personal integrity naturally develops.

Thus, often, the first stage in kung fu training is to experience being hit without reacting in anger or with the intention of revenge. The goal is to deflate the ego. Ego interferes with learning and with the development of virtue. Once you accept being hit, you will learn to dodge, to think clearly, to respond immediately and effectively to any attack, be it physical, verbal, or emotional. In this way you develop self-control. Ironically, in becoming stronger, the true kung fu master also becomes better able and more inclined to handle situations appropriately and effectively without using force.

Ego interferes with personal development; let it go, and virtue automatically develops.

Thus internal training, while perhaps the least spectacular and dramatic aspect of your kung fu training, is nevertheless absolutely essential and worthy of your full devotion. Give attention to the three aspects: internal energy, disciplining your mind and emotion, and developing virtue. In particular, meditation of some sort will help in all three; there are many forms, and all work. In developing discipline and concentration, you will also develop virtue—the power to use your techniques, as well as *not* to use your techniques, which is the true spirit of the martial arts.

safety

A T THE BEGINNING LEVELS of kung fu, you will not be using weapons, and you are unlikely to engage in sparring (contact with another person). Thus, any injuries and/or pain you may experience are most likely to be the result of misuse or overuse of a body part. The bad news is that almost everyone practicing a martial art suffers some kind of problem—if only a sore muscle now and then. The good news is that most serious injury can be avoided by following certain precautions and using common sense.

The first section below suggests ways to prevent injury, while the other sections deals with ways to treat some of the more common, simple, and mild injuries. *In all cases, if you suspect a serious problem is developing or has occurred, see a qualified doctor.*

Is Kung fu Dangerous?

K ung fu is relatively safe, especially at the beginning level. As a beginner you will probably do only hand forms—no weapons, no sparring. The most frequent injuries at this level are self-inflicted: muscle strains and joint injuries.

Prevention

Prevention is always better than cure. Damage to muscles, bones, or joints can occur in a split second and then take weeks, if not months, to heal. All that recovery time may teach you valuable lessons about patience, but it will be a trial for both body and mind. Rather than risk permanent damage and rather than waste valuable time recovering from temporary damage, try to avoid injury altogether.

1.   First, warm up. As described more fully in chapter 12: "Warming Up," gradually bring your body into gear either by following the routine of your school or by using a routine of your own. The body is like a rubber band. When warm, it is pliable and resilient. When cold, it tends to be stiff and brittle, so that any sudden or extreme motion can cause some part of it to tear, break, or snap. The strategy, then, is to get the blood moving, loosen the joints, warm and stretch the muscles, and *then* begin serious training. This will not only prevent injury but will enable you to practice longer with better results.

2. **Stop before damage occurs.** The second cardinal rule for avoiding injury is to stop when you *begin* to feel pain or discomfort, not *after* damage occurs. When you feel discomfort, stop to make sure you are doing the movement correctly. Ask your teacher or a senior student to watch you, and then correct any problems they can see. This is particularly true for movements involving the knees. If the feet and knees are not properly aligned, or if weight is not distributed properly, damage to ligaments and joints can easily—and quickly—occur. Sometimes pain is simply a sign that muscles are being challenged beyond their usual limits, and you can safely train "through" it. At other times, pain warns that damage has occurred or is likely to occur. Pay attention to your own body; learn to recognize the difference between a challenge and a red alert!

3. **Go slowly.** When learning any new technique or form, practice slowly and deliberately at first. Make sure you are doing it absolutely correctly before trying to do it quickly or powerfully. Many of the movements require subtle shifts of weight or movements of the torso; if you miss these movements, you can twist or strain other parts of the body as they try to compensate. This is particularly true for jumping kicks and low movements requiring squatting on one leg. By going slowly at first, you will not only avoid injury, but also thoroughly develop your skill and understanding of the movement so that, when done quickly, the movement will not only be safe but also easier and more graceful.

4. **Eat sensibly.** As with any other vigorous exercise, do not eat a heavy meal just before coming to a workout. It is best to eat at least an hour before exercise and to wait at least an hour after vigorous exercise before eating a heavy meal. The stomach is a muscle too; when it is full, it must work—if you try to do vigorous exercise with other muscles, a conflict develops that could result in discomfort, cramps, and worse. Eat well during the day, and you will have plenty of good energy to sustain you through the workout.

Note: Traditional kung fu masters discouraged students from eating or drinking during or immediately following a workout as they believed it interfered with the circulation of qi.

5. **Drink sensibly.** "Sensibly" refers not only to what to drink but also how and when to drink. Keeping your body well hydrated will prevent injury by keeping your muscles in top condition and by keeping your mind working clearly. But drinking too much or taking cold liquids could hinder rather than help. The first suggestion is to drink water. You may drink other liquids as well—but always drink water. (Try water with a slice of lime or lemon in it, if you find plain water hard to swallow.) Second, it is highly recommended that you drink liquids at room temperature—neither very hot nor very cold. This is classic Chinese advice, and although it runs counter to the habits of most Americans today, it makes good sense. In particular, taking anything cold into your body when you are hot shocks the system and actually interferes with your body's ability to absorb what it needs as quickly as possible. Finally, when you are panting or if your heart is pounding heavily, do not drink: instead, merely rinse your mouth with water or take only a few sips at a time. When your heart pounds, your body is under stress; taking a lot of liquid into your stomach at the same time will only cause more stress. The best strategy is to make sure you are well hydrated *before* your workout, and then to sip room temperature water as needed during and until about half an hour after your workout.

6. **Cool down.** After every workout, spend a few minutes stretching and relaxing. (See chapter 12) This will help your muscles recover from strain (clearing lactic acid and other metabolic residues from the tissues), dispel tension, allow your body to restore its energy and recover its equilibrium—and thereby prevent injury. It is not a waste of time.

7. **Rest between workouts.** This means not only to rest your whole body, but also to rest the parts of your body that have been working the hardest. The older you are, the longer you may need for recovery. Alternate workouts and types of exercise that stress different parts of the body. In that way the body can recover and rebuild itself; you will be building it up, not wearing it down.

Injuries

Common Injuries

Most of the injuries martial artists suffer—and especially beginning martial artists—have to do with muscles, bones, and joints. The four most common types of pain and/or injury are strain (pulled muscle), sprain (stretched or torn ligament), overuse, and hyperextension injuries. Knees are by far the most common site of pain and injury, with shoulders, elbows, and lower back next. As you practice, treat all of these areas with particular respect, and take care of any problems at the beginning, when they are small and less severe.

We repeat: If there is any question as to whether an injury is serious, see a doctor.

1. **Strains.** Also called a "pulled muscle," muscle strain occurs when a muscle (or tendon, which is tissue connecting muscle to bone) is stretched beyond its usual range of motion. It usually happens suddenly, with pain, tenderness, and swelling. Usually the muscle gets sore but continues to function. If, instead, it doesn't seem to work at all, more serious damage could have occurred, and you should seek medical help immediately.

   In the case of ordinary muscle soreness, rest and ice will usually restore the muscle within a day or two. Recovery from a serious muscle strain is more likely to take a week or two, depending on the size of the muscle involved, and the person.

   To prevent strains, warm-ups and stretching before workouts and weight training/conditioning exercises are highly recommended.

2. **Sprains.** Whereas a strain involves muscle tissue, a sprain involves ligaments, the tissues that connect bones to bones. Usually sprains occur suddenly, as the result of a misstep, twist, or fall. The affected area will suddenly swell and become very painful. Mild sprains usually heal on thier own, but a severe sprain could involve a fracture or dislocation of the bones at the joint. If

Strain versus Sprain

A strain involves muscle tissue; a sprain involves ligaments. Strains usually heal in a few days; sprains can require weeks, if not months, to heal.

a snapping or popping sound is heard when the injury occurs, seek medical help immediately because the ligament may have actually detached, or been torn, from the bone.

In the case of ordinary sprains, as with strains, rest and ice will usually help. However, sprains take longer to heal: You may be able to put weight on the affected part after a day or two, but recovery could take four to six weeks, due to the relatively low blood supply to ligaments. Thus, you should continue to treat the affected part with care for at least a month. If you become active too soon, the joint won't heal properly and will remain weak—thus increasing the chance of reinjury, but with a more severe injury the second time around. You may want to consider visiting a physical therapist to make sure the ligament heals completely and is truly as good as new.

3. **Overuse Injuries.** This category covers pain that usually develops gradually in a joint or ligament that is used repetitively—especially if that part of the body has not been used much before. Examples are tendonitis and bursitis. To prevent such injuries, stretch thoroughly before a workout. If such a condition begins to develop, first check with your instructor to be sure you are performing movements correctly; be particularly sensitive to how you are using your hips and shoulders. Rest the area; apply ice to reduce inflammation. If the condition continues, consult a sports trainer or doctor; anti-inflammatory medicines or even some physical therapy may be recommended.

4. **Hyperextension Injuries.** Hyperextension injuries happen in a flash, when a joint is forced to move beyond its normal range of motion. After a strong kick or punch, if you suddenly experience pain that then persists whenever you use that limb or joint, you may have a case of hyperextension. To recover, rest and use ice and other anti-inflammatory measures; if the pain persists, see a doctor.

These injuries probably most often occur when a person kicks or punches into the air—as opposed to using a bag or other target. A target will stop the forward motion and absorb the force, whereas a punch into the air can put full stress on a joint. Thus, to avoid hyperextension when practicing without a target, never use full force, and always keep the punching or kicking limb slightly bent.

The I.C.E.R. Treatment

For minor, simple bone and soft-tissue injuries, a standard procedure for care is summarized in the acronym I.C.E.R., which stands for "ice - compression - elevation - rest"—applied in that order. It is also often referred to, and perhaps more easily remembered, as R.I.C.E.

> I.C.E.R., or R.I.C.E., is the standard treatment for simple injuries:
>
> ☞ Ice
>
> ☞ Compression
>
> ☞ Elevation
>
> ☞ Rest

1. **Ice.** The first step is to apply ice. For either a strain or sprain, tissues are damaged, and blood and fluids will be seeping from broken vessels into the site of the injury, causing swelling. Cold will cause the broken vessels to constrict and will numb nerve endings, thus reducing swelling and pain. Three rules when applying ice: First, don't apply ice directly to the skin. Instead, wrap it in a cloth and then apply it to the injured site. Second, apply ice intermittently—off and on, with longer periods off than on. Third, don't apply ice continuously for more than twenty minutes. For example, apply an ice pack for fifteen minutes, then rest without it for forty-five minutes. This particularly helps at the early stage of an injury. How long to use the ice treatment? Most authorities agree that you should continue to apply ice off and on for seventy-two hours after an injury, or at least until the swelling goes down. After the swelling is completely gone (and some authorities recommend not before seven days, even when the swelling subsides earlier), then you may apply heat in order to speed tissue repair.

2. **Compression.** To help reduce pain and provide support to the swollen area, you may also want to apply compression, by wrapping the injured site until swelling subsides. Just be careful not to wrap so tightly as to restrict blood flow and cause other problems.

3. **Elevation.** When possible, elevate the injury to reduce blood flow (and therefore swelling). This will also reduce pain and improve blood circulation, improving healing. Ideally, keep the affected part above the level of the heart. At night you may use a pillow or folded blanket to protect the area and to keep it raised.

4. **Rest.** Finally, rest both the whole body and, especially, the injured body part, until healing is well under way. Go slowly in resuming your previous level of activity. If an injured body part is allowed to heal com-

pletely, it can be as good as new. If not, it will be more prone to injury, and the second time, the damage is likely to be much worse, if not permanent. Complete healing could take weeks, so continue to protect and favor an injured limb well past the point when it *seems* to be well.

Soreness without Injury

If you have no injury, but your muscles are simply sore, tight, or stiff, then the question of inflammation determines what you should do. Heat causes expansion and relaxation; coolness (ice) causes contraction. Thus, if there is any inflammation, apply ice. If there is simply tightness, then apply a moist heat pack (moist heat penetrates deeper than dry) or heat rub. A hot bath or hot water soak (some people like to add epsom salts for greater effect) can help. A medicated liniment for muscle soreness, or a Chinese dit da jow (see below), may also speed healing.

Finally, always remember: Whenever any part of your body is stiff or sore, take time to warm it thoroughly and bring it into action gently.

Dit Da Jow or Tie Da Jiu

The time-honored Chinese treatment for muscle aches and pains of martial artists is herbal extracts, known collectively as dit da jow (Cantonese) or *tie da jiu* (Mandarin), which can be roughly translated as "hit-fall wine." In the past,

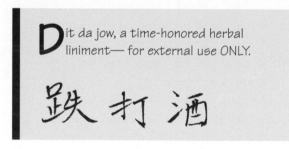

Dit da jow, a time-honored herbal liniment— for external use ONLY.

many kung fu sifus were also medical doctors and made dit da jow for their students, using either their own or inherited (and usually secret) formulas. Such medicines were used not only to heal but also to prevent injury, particularly for body parts to be toughened by repeated striking. For example, iron palm training involves repeated striking of the hand on objects of increasing hardness. Before each session of training, special medicine was, is, and should be applied that penetrates skin and tissue down to the bone, toughening and conditioning the striking area, maintaining circulation, and effectively preventing bruises, calluses, and deformity.

Some traditional kung fu sifus still make their own dit da jow. If this is true in your school, ask an instructor where it is and how to use it. If not, then commercial versions are available on the Web and possibly from martial arts supply stores.

With dit da jow and similar medicated liniments, the general procedure is to apply a small amount and rub thoroughly into the painful area. They are dark in color and may stain clothing, so beware of this possible disadvantage. Wash your hands after using the liniment, be sure not to get it near your eyes, do not get it into open wounds, and never take it internally.

Cramps

A final category of pain that might occur is muscle cramp. Sudden, sharp pain, especially associated with a hard lump of muscle tissue that can be seen or felt, often indicates a cramp. This can be caused by fatigue, dehydration, or mineral imbalance or deficiency, affecting the nerve tissue. To treat a cramp, massage the affected area, applying heat and pressure, until the muscle tissue relaxes. Then, rest, drink liquids at room temperature, and stretch the muscle gently and thoroughly before resuming your workout.

To prevent cramps, stay hydrated, stretch thoroughly before every workout, and make sure your diet is well balanced in minerals. If the cramps occur frequently, you may want to consult a doctor, as sometimes other internal factors can cause cramps.

part 5

making progress

THESE LAST CHAPTERS present an overview of the more advanced stages of your kung fu studies, beyond the beginning three to six months.

After you become familiar with your school and settle into training, you will first need to develop a long-term program—a regimen that will see you through inevitable lapses in dedication and ensure that you achieve results. Second, you will need some way to measure your progress—some way to know that you are indeed moving forward toward your goals. Finally, as a member of a school, you may be asked or have the opportunity to participate in a competition or demonstration. The last chapter offers tips on what to expect and how to prepare for those eventualities.

chapter 18
your training
program

To ACHIEVE you must first have a goal. Then you must have a method. Third, you need criteria for judging how you are progressing, so that you can adjust your methods to stay on track. Finally, you need patience and persistence to stick with it. You may call these elements, all together, a training program. They will work for virtually any goal you have in your life.

A training program in kung fu should include these basic pairs of elements:

✦ Drills (that is, repetitive exercises that build strength, flexibility, and endurance) and forms (that is, practice in performing the techniques in continuous, nonstop sequences)

✦ Group work (especially in learning applications) and solo work (necessary for you to make sure you have thoroughly understood the exercises and can do them on your own)

✦ External, physical work as well as internal, mental training

But first, you must set the "budget" for your program.

How Much Time and Effort Can You Afford to Spend?

Personal Considerations

To establish a training program in kung fu, start with your own personal goals. Knowing what you want to get out of kung fu will help you determine how much you want to put into it. Why are you studying it? What do you want to accomplish? Are you after health and fitness? Are you studying because you want to learn how to punch and kick like a kung fu movie star? Or do you mainly want to learn some self-defense techniques?

A second, very closely related, aspect of goals is how to measure your progress. How will you judge whether your training program is working and whether progress is fast enough? Understanding your motives and knowing how you will gauge progress will enable you to focus your training program so that you see results and feel satisfied with your efforts.

A third aspect to consider is your priorities. How important is kung fu compared to the other activities in your life? You also have other responsibilities and interests—career, family, friends, and hobbies. Where does kung fu fit into the whole picture? This question will probably lead you back to goals—but in the broader picture of your whole life. What do you want to accomplish in

If you give it priority, studying kung fu can improve every aspect of your life.

your life, and how do the small parts of your life contribute to that larger picture? Your attitude is all-important here. Kung fu can be a big or small part of your life. You can treat it as simply physical exercise, or you can use it as a tool for self -development, building not only body, but also mind and spirit, developing the muscles to punch and kick, but also—and more importantly—the power *not* to punch and kick, and the will, confidence, and self-discipline to resolve problems peacefully. This is the original and true purpose of kung fu. Thus, sincere study of kung fu has the power to improve virtually every aspect of your life, but to realize that potential you must give kung fu priority in your life—starting with your training program.

Scheduling

Having examined your goals in taking up kung fu and having considered them in relation to the other goals in your life, next look at your schedule. How much time are you willing to devote to attending class? How often and how long can you practice at home? When will you practice? Adding something new to your schedule means you will have to eliminate or shorten the time you spend on something else; what will kung fu replace? Be realistic. From the beginning, set a training schedule that you believe you can stick to—right now.

Give it a good shot for, say, three months; then reassess and possibly adjust. This too will help guarantee that you see results, feel satisfied, and accomplish what you set out to do.

Beginners often ask, "How often should I come to class? Should I work out at home? How long should I work out?" While the answers vary with the individual, experienced sifus tend to agree about some general guidelines that they have seen hold true for most people.

First, to maintain consistent development of your muscles, to keep what you have learned fresh in your mind, and to see progress quickly, the ideal schedule is to join workout sessions or classes at the school three times a week. In this way, your body can take a day of rest between hard workouts, but your mind will not forget what you have learned. If you practice at the school, the instructors will be able to catch your mistakes early and correct them before they become ingrained habits. When you commit to a class at the school (a place dedicated to just this work, where there are other people devoting their time to it), you are more likely to do the workout than if you have to rely on your own self-discipline for a workout at home.

How Often Do I Need to Practice?

For best results, attend three workouts per week at the school.

Second best is coming to the school two times a week. Again, at that frequency, what you are learning will be fresh in your mind, and your body will be building muscle and coordination, so you will make noticeable progress. Some instructors feel that twice a week is the minimum to maintain momentum in your studies.

Coming only once a week is discouraged, unless you practice diligently at home between classes. The major problem with coming so infrequently is that you tend to forget what you have learned at the previous class. Thus, every time you come, you must spend a good deal of time reviewing what you learned rather than moving forward. This is particularly discouraging if other members of the class are coming more frequently. With more frequent repetition, not only will they remember better, but they will simply be able to do it better as well. You will feel even worse. And this could lead you to lose interest and drop out of the class altogether.

If you work out regularly—no matter how often, whether at home or at the school—you will make progress. Such effort is never wasted. But for noticeable results and to maintain your motivation (and your self-esteem in class), try to attend class or work out on your own three times a week.

Besides how often you will work out, a second and equally important consideration is when you will work out. Morning, evening, during lunch—the time does not matter as much as the commitment. Decide when you will work

How Long Does it Take to be Good?

That depends on many factors, and especially on what you mean by "good." If you mean feeling as if you are getting the hang of it, then if you attend class regularly, two or three times per week, you should see results in about six months. To achieve any level of mastery requires years of dedicated practice.

out, and then stick to it. This is where attending a class has psychological advantages over the commitment to practice on your own. The class time is fixed, and you have paid for it. So there is no decision to be made as to when practice will be, or how long, and there is less room for mental negotiation.

In contrast, when you practice on your own, there is more risk that your will power will fail or that other commitments and sudden complications will interfere. Again, you must be realistic about yourself, your other commitments, and your schedule. For most people, the early morning hours before work are the best for exercise. They are fresh from a night's sleep, and no other responsibilities are likely to interfere—no telephone calls or meetings or appointments. The biggest hurdle could be getting out of bed! In that case, you must make a firm resolve, and then create incentives that will ensure that you stick to your workout schedule.

Seasonal Considerations

In the past in China, martial artists were advised to take advantage of the seasons for vigorous training. That is, during warm weather, the body is naturally more limber and flexible, so training is faster and you can achieve results

Adapt your training schedule to natural energies—both your own and those of the seasons.

in almost half the time it takes during colder weather. So, in those days before central heating, training began in April or May, continued intensively during the following three or four months, and finished in August. To achieve the same results during the fall and winter took seven or eight months.

With modern warm buildings and in warmer climates, this same advice may not apply, but it is nonetheless worth considering as you set your own training schedule. Working with, rather than against, natural energies seems to be good common sense, and will probably "feel" better as well. Thus, you may go easy in the colder months, and then when the spring arrives, use the surging energy of the season to fuel your own training program.

Workout Structure

The structure of every workout for any level of training is basically the same; however, the emphasis differs according to the stage of learning.

Every workout should, or is likely to, include the following elements:

Warm-up exercises

Drills

Strength and endurance training

Forms

(Free-sparring)

Cool-down

(Meditation)

Each workout will naturally begin with warm-ups and end with cool-down exercises, and possibly a meditation. As for the other elements, the order and amount of time spent on each will vary with the school and, particularly, with the stage of the students' learning.

In the beginning, for new students, drills are emphasized. These drills build—and, later, maintain—the muscles and skills that are the root, the core, and the foundation of everything that kung fu is about. Its beauty, power, and effectiveness all derive from mastery of the basic stances and hand and foot techniques. Thus, instructors will insist that beginners concentrate on these drills in order to build muscles, increase strength and endurance, and develop coordination and balance. Students must learn to assume the various postures and stances correctly and automatically, without thinking. In addition, they must simply become familiar with the name of each stance and movement. The simplicity of these drills also helps students to purify their minds and concentrate. Thus, they are good for students who are beginning their training, but they are also good for every student at the beginning of every training session. Focus and concentration ensure that students will derive maximum benefit from their workout time.

Strength and endurance training are also important at this stage. There are many ways to build muscles and increase endurance. Jumping rope, push-ups, weightlifting, chin-ups, using gym equipment or your own body—all methods work. And most schools of kung fu have their own traditional methods, especially for developing the specific muscles needed for the characteristic hand or foot forms of their school. (See Chapter 14, "Drills and Conditioning Exercises.") To set your own training program in this aspect, consult your instructor. He or she will be able to guide you in the right direction, and also at the right speed.

> In the beginning, drills are emphasized to build muscles as well as muscle memory.

> At the next stage, simple forms are taught to develop the students' flexibility and fluidity in connecting the movements in a series, as in a real fight.

> As students progress, more advanced forms are taught, as well as two-person sparring forms and weapons forms.

At the next stage, students begin to learn forms. That is, after learning the basic movements and developing some skill in executing them, beginners will go on to learn simple forms. The forms challenge the student to move cleanly and quickly from one stance or movement to another. The first forms taught will be simple and short; again, unfamiliar patterns and concepts will be introduced gradually, so that the student will continue to develop a strong foundation and a core understanding of the art.

After simple forms have been mastered, students progress to longer and more complex forms, including two-person forms. In addition, students who have mastered the basic elements and their applications will take up free-sparring. At this point, most students also begin to learn weapons forms, beginning with the wooden staff and progressively working up to sabers and swords.

While broadening their technique, students will also be deepening it. Instructors will emphasize the applications of the various movements of the forms—that is, how a particular movement should be executed in terms of the action of an invisible opponent. Instructors will also emphasize subtleties of the movements; with months, if not years, of training, advanced students will then appreciate fine points they were previously unaware of and then face the challenge of learning to do these moves themselves.

Thus, the training program is dynamic, determined by the school, the students' natures, and the level of study. While at the school, you will follow the

Practice on your own, but practice only what you know.

instructor and the class. While at home, you should follow the routine of the class as far as you can. Practicing on your own is a good challenge to the memory and will greatly improve your mental mastery of what you are learning. But, in all cases, practice only what you know. If you are unsure of how to do a move or sequence, then leave it until the next class. Try to avoid developing a bad habit. If you find you have trouble remembering, then during the next class, simply focus on one or two movements or parts of forms; be absolutely certain you understand and do them correctly, then practice them until the next class. Such effort is never wasted.

Mature and Not-Quite-Fit Students

Kung fu is suitable for people of all ages; however, all people should train according to their disposition and their physical condition. Past the age of thirty, physical fitness can be more a question of exercise habits, diet, and daily care than of age; people of fifty can be more fit than people of forty, depending on how they take care of themselves.

Nevertheless, there are a few basic principles and words of advice that will apply to older people (and younger people who are not quite fit!) as they take up kung fu for the first time. The first, and most important, principle is to go slowly. Spend more time warming up and stretching, as well as cooling down. Tackle new techniques and forms methodically and slowly. Be content to develop flexibility gradually. Be patient, as it will naturally take your body longer to do everything—from developing power and flexibility to recovering from exercise. Concentrate on what you are doing, performing each move-

Am I Too Old for Kung fu?

No. If you want to train, you can. But older students need to train differently than teenagers. Choose the school, style, and forms that suit you. Older people have certain advantages over younger students: They typically have more discipline, dedication, and determination (that is, they know what they want and are willing to work for it). They grasp the subtleties more quickly (in other words, they can see beyond punching and kicking). Also, remember that kung fu trains qualities of mind and spirit that are good for anyone at any age.

ment accurately and precisely. Speed will come later. Second, in learning techniques, focus on the basics, rather than the dramatic frills. That is, don't try to perform the dramatic jumps, lunges, and deep stances favored by younger people. Instead, concentrate on solid basic stances, balance, and coordination. In fact, this is where the real power and beauty of kung fu come from, so such effort will be well rewarded. Third, exercise moderately. In doing basic stances, take higher body positions in the beginning, then gradually lower your weight to increase the intensity of the exercise. Do not overdo it; do not strain or exhaust yourself.

Finally, take heart by acknowledging your strengths. Older people tend to have more staying power, greater faculty of understanding, and an advantage in absolute strength. Accept both your strengths and your weaknesses, and use them like tools to achieve your goals.

Overcoming Discouragement

Almost every student faces discouragement within the first six months of training. After the thrill of joining the school wears off and the drudgery of training sets in, almost everyone begins to wonder whether they are wasting their time. "Is this worth it?" they ask themselves. "Am I really learning anything? How come I'm not learning what I wanted to learn?" These sorts of thoughts not only interfere with concentration, but they also interfere with physical performance. As the mind loses concentration, the student finds it harder to remember what is taught, and this makes the body move stiffly. It is important to confront discouragement as soon as it appears. Generally, such thoughts will trail off in one of three directions as students seek the cause of their dissatisfaction:

1. People blame themselves. "I'm really not cut out for this; I can't learn very well, and I'm not nearly as good as everyone else. I should quit and stop embarrassing myself."
2. People blame their instructor. "He doesn't like me," or "She's ignoring me. " "He's not teaching me very well, and/or he's not teaching me what I really came here to learn." "She really doesn't care."
3. People blame the school. "This is not a very good school. I should have gone to a bigger/smaller school, or a school of karate/judo/aikido, and so on." "People here really aren't very good or very friendly."

If—or when!—you encounter such thoughts, you may want to consider the following before you act.

First, honestly determine whether the main problem is that you are simply impatient—that is, you are disappointed in how little you have learned in the time you have been practicing. The antidote to this is to reexamine your

When discouraged, avoid blame. Just work harder.

expectations in terms of how long you have been practicing, especially in view of your age and fitness when you started. Are your expectations realistic? Just as a new piano student cannot expect to play Beethoven after six weeks of study, neither can a kung fu student expect to kick and punch like Jackie Chan after only a short period of study. Younger people and people who enter the school already fit will naturally "catch on" more quickly. Their bodies will be used to learning new ways to move, and they will have the muscles and the cardiovascular endurance to practice longer. This does not mean that older and less fit people should not try! On the contrary, they will benefit far more in the long run, but it will take time. In the beginning it may seem like an impossible task. Don't be discouraged. Instead, just be realistic about what you have achieved, and what you can expect to have achieved, given your level of fitness and effort. Also, remember that the greatest benefit from kung fu may not be in the physical exercise, but rather in the mental discipline required to persevere, to concentrate, and—inevitably, then—to achieve.

Second, remember that the human learning curve is not a smooth, continuous upward slope; instead, people typically learn in spurts, followed by a plateau when they don't seem to be learning anything, and then suddenly another growth/learning spurt comes. This could be your case. After intense

> **T**rue achievement should be measured not by the level you attain but by how much you progress.

learning and progress in the beginning, you may have hit a plateau. This does not mean that you have stopped learning; it just means your body is adjusting and developing toward another spurt, which is coming later. Be patient.

Learning is cyclical. Keep working, and you will progress.

Third, reassure yourself of the value of foundation drills. If you are discontented with unending repetitions of seemingly boring exercises, remember that *this* is the way the body learns. Only by these endless repetitions will your body learn to perform these movements accurately, quickly, smoothly, powerfully. You should perform drills as precisely and accurately as forms, and with as much attention as you pay to the forms, even though the forms may seem more interesting and more important. Remind yourself that what you are doing is of critical importance. Without a strong root, the tree falls.

Learning is repetition—life is repetition! Breathe in, breathe out; there is no escape. Just be present in the moment.

If you think the problem is that you are much worse than other students and seem to be wasting the sifu's time because you don't learn fast enough, calm your mind. The sifu has seen hundreds of students, and you are unlikely to be the worst (or the best) of all of them. Furthermore, the sifu is not looking for skill, but for perseverance, dedication, respect for the art, and the will to

Slow learners often learn more thoroughly. Slow and steady wins in the long run.

succeed. He or she knows that fast learners sometimes don't learn thoroughly, while slow learners, who must repeat every movement a thousand times, are more likely to master the technique in the long run. And the sifu is definitely in this for the long run. Your sifu will be teaching you slowly and patiently and will expect you simply to do your best: that ensures success for both you and your teacher.

If you think the problem is that the sifu doesn't like you, or doesn't care about your progress, you should recognize that the chances of this are low. Teachers who do not want their students to succeed are extremely rare. Also, remember that kung fu sifus are traditionally rigorous and demanding with everyone, especially with students they feel have potential. That is, the sifu might make the best students work harder, trying to develop them to their fullest potential. Metal must be ground and polished and tempered before it becomes fine steel. By *not* showering you with praise and attention, the sifu could be testing your "mettle": What kind of person are you? Can you persevere and work on your own? Or do you need to be mollycoddled and treated with special attention? Again, the value of kung fu is in mental and spiritual as well as physical development, and the sifu's attitude is part of your training too.

The true kung fu artist will be immune to both praise and insult. Make your mind as steady and solid as your horse stance.

Finally, if your discouragement and dissatisfaction boil down to discontent with the school and not just with your level of progress, then you should consider two aspects. First, examine why you have this idea. Is it because of something someone said to you? Do your friends seem to be having a better time at another school? Or maybe you don't like the other students at your school? Is it something about the attitude of the sifu and the senior students? In this case, the best course of action is to wait at least six months, and then reconsider. Kung fu is a lifelong pursuit, and it is traditionally a lifelong commitment to a sifu. To make progress, you must get along with your sifu, and you must respect and honor him or her, perhaps even more than a parent. Similarly, you must get along with the senior students, because they will be teaching you and helping you along as much as the sifu. Furthermore, the senior students reflect some of the quality and nature of the sifu, especially if they have been with this teacher for more than ten years, as is common in good schools. Both the sifu and senior students should be honest, dedicated, friendly, and helpful—as

> ### I'm OK—
> ### But the School is Not!
>
> Suspend judgment for at least six months. Work diligently; do your best. Then, after six months, you will have the experience and knowledge to decide whether you really should switch schools.

well as skilled in their art. They are your role models. If, after six months, you feel that these are not people you can admire, nor people whom you would want to emulate, then it is perhaps wise to look elsewhere.

It should be noted here that, while most students' dissatisfaction and discouragement come from impatience, for some it could in fact be a mismatch of student and school. You might have made a wrong choice—especially if you are a rank beginner, just starting out in kung fu without experience or knowledge, and you chose the school from an advertisement rather than a personal recommendation. In that case, work diligently for at least six months, and then begin to check out other schools. With your experience at the first school, you will have a much better idea how to evaluate a school and be able to choose more wisely.

Mind over Matter

In all cases, when you feel discouraged, try to examine the situation realistically and rationally. Do not give in to emotions, and never act when you are under their influence. Instead, decide that you will suspend judgment for at least six months. During this time, do not compare yourself with others; do not harbor unrealistic expectations; do not question the quality of your instructor or the school. Simply work diligently, concentrate on what you are learning, and do your best. Then, at the end of six months, assess how you feel and what you have accomplished, and consider the school and its sifu and students. *Then* decide how best to pursue your goals.

This too is part of kung fu training.

chapter 19

gauging progress

AVING UNDERTAKEN the study of kung fu, how do you gauge your progress? The answer comes from both within and without.

Testing for Promotion

While formal ranking is not part of traditional martial arts, today most kung fu/ wushu schools have some kind of regular testing program by which students can demonstrate and certify progressive mastery of the art. A few schools use a colored belt system, as in karate; many schools award certificates.

Whether to test or not to test and the form of the testing varies dramatically between schools and styles, because kung fu is essentially unorganized. While

esting has always been the domain of individual kung fu schools; formal ranking systems are a modern phenomenon.

wushu is somewhat centralized, with an international organization headquartered in China, no such organization exists for kung fu. Some of the styles have formally organized into federations or associations with rules and systems for ranking. Otherwise, individual sifus set up and run their schools more or less as they like or according to the traditions of their particular sifus and kung fu styles. Similarly, the cost of any testing in these programs differs and is determined by the school or an organization to which the school belongs.

At one end of the spectrum, some kung fu schools have a testing program as rigorous and organized as in karate or taekwondo. This mainly applies to large, modern schools where most of the students are children. Such schools usually organize formal testing sessions on a regular basis, every three to six months. The sifu will invite students he or she feels are ready to register to be tested. Students pay a fee to be tested, whether or not they pass. Judges are the

senior students and/or sifu; in schools
that belong to a larger organization or
federation, sifus from other schools may
be asked to come to act as judges. All
students will be expected to attend as
audience, and family and friends of can-
didates being tested will also be invited

> In schools with testing programs, the requirements for passing each level will be clearly specified.

to attend. Usually students perform individually. The atmosphere is formal,
and students are expected to treat the occasion seriously, whether performing
or not.

The test for each level is a form from the repertory of the school's style of
kung fu. The forms are progressively more difficult; at higher levels, there may
be weapons and two-person forms. Requirements for the different levels are
clearly specified and taught to the students. A beginning student can expect to
be ready for the first test after approximately three months. Timing of subsequent tests will depend heavily on how often and how diligently the student
practices. And it will also depend on the school's attitude toward tests. The sifu
may have found that the students like or need frequent tests to give them
incentive to practice harder. In other schools the number of levels and tests
may be fewer and, naturally, in that case, more significant.

At the other end of the spectrum—at smaller and more traditional schools—
there is no formal testing program. These sorts of schools usually cater to
more mature students. In these schools students simply study and learn
according to the sifu's instruction. Their own internal assessment of their
progress and achievement is enough incentive to keep up the practice. In addition, they get an idea of how well they are doing by what the sifu chooses to
teach them and how fast it is taught. That is, some forms are considered to be
more difficult or challenging then others. Hence, when the sifu begins teach-

The level of difficulty of the form you are learning is also a measure of
your progress.

ing them these forms, students understand that they have achieved a certain
level of competence.

In between these two extremes of the large school with a formal testing program and the small school with no certificates, there is a huge variety.

Again, how the system works at any individual school is largely determined by the sifu of the school. When you join a school you should ask—or you will be told—how the system works at that school. (Indeed, this may be one of the criteria for choosing a school: those people who do not like public performances will be better off avoiding schools with rigorous testing programs, while those people who like certificates and clear evidence of their achievements will do best to choose such schools.)

Preparation for Testing

If your school has a testing program, here are a few words of advice for preparing and performing. First, remember that the purpose of the test is to help you improve your skill; it is not to torture you! Keep this in mind, and use every aspect of test preparation to make your form better.

Begin by knowing the form you will be tested on, inside and out. You might want to perform it for your family or friends before the testing session, in order to get practice in doing it as a performance in front of other people. If having people watch unnerves you, getting used to this can help you do better during the test. If you have any questions at all, ask beforehand. Again, performing for an audience of friends before the test may bring out your weak points or points you are not sure about. When you feel uncertainty, ask. This will not only help you succeed at the test, but also improve your form.

For the test, make sure your kung fu uniform is clean and pressed. Make sure you are clean and rested!

On the day of the test, treat your performance as a typical workout session. Prepare by doing your typical warm-up routine. Not only will this get you physically ready, but the familiar routine should also help calm your nerves. Avoid talking; instead, keep your mind focused on what you are about to do.

Testing can be an important means of gauging progress and renewing motivation. Use it to your advantage—do not view it as a torture.

During the test—during your performance—be on your best behavior. Every moment that you are on view, maintain good posture, keep quiet, and show respect to your sifu, your school, the judges, the audience, your art, and yourself.

Finally, enjoy the process. Here is your chance to show your sifu, your parents, and your friends what you have achieved. They are there to help you celebrate the fruits of long hours of work and dedication.

Home Videos

One means of measuring progress that some students find extremely helpful is home-video recording. With a simple tripod and camcorder, you can even film yourself practicing forms. This has several valuable benefits. First, it gives you the experience of "performing." Even though you are recording only for your own viewing, nevertheless, there is a certain tension created by awareness of the camera's eye. This helps develop concentration. Second, it enables you to see yourself as others see you. This can be quite a shock! How you feel doing a form can be quite different from how you look doing a form. By making a film of yourself, you can compare how you look with how others look, rather than comparing how you feel with how others look. When you *see* your mistakes, you may be better able to correct them. In this case, seeing is certainly believing, and students who watch themselves often then tackle their workouts with renewed dedication, determination, and understanding of what they are trying to accomplish.

> Home videos give you the experience of performing, enable you to see your mistakes as others do, and document your level for future comparison.

The third value of home videos is as a record of your progress. If you make a video of yourself every several months, you will have a clear record of how you are improving. Begin perhaps a month after you join the school. Put that video away. Then six months later, make another video. If you have been working regularly and diligently, the change will surely surprise and please you.

Inner Progress

Even without a belt or a certificate or a home video, you should be able to feel the progress you are making. First, you should feel your body getting stronger, the movements becoming easier to do, the sessions becoming invigorating rather than exhausting. Every once in a while, you may feel the flow of a movement within a form, as the power of a block or punch naturally melts into the next movement. This is a sign that you are "getting it." Second, you may sense a change in your personality and in your life. As people progress in kung fu, they typically become more patient, more self-confident, more even-tempered, and more humble. The more you learn, the more you understand how much you still have to learn. The more you practice, the deeper your concentration will become. The more you watch, the more you will see the subtleties of movements that totally escaped your awareness before. Then, having seen these subtleties, you will be challenged to be able to do them yourself. In this ongoing process there is meaning, satisfaction, and self-fulfillment. These qualities will reverberate throughout your life.

chapter 20

competitions and
demonstrations

WHILE KUNG FU is essentially a fighting art, it has also been a performing art from its earliest days. In the Tang and Song dynasties, people earned their livings as street performers of certain martial arts forms. Later, when the Manchus forbade the native Han from carrying weapons, martial arts techniques were preserved and practiced in disguise, as part of operatic performances. Crowds gathered to admire the speed, grace, and agility of these artists, as well as their power and prowess.

The tradition lingers. Today many martial arts schools send teams to participate in parades or perform at public events. In Chinese communities, kung fu schools may be asked to perform the lion dance at festivals, openings, or private events. In addition to performances, there are now numerous local, national, and international tournaments and competitions where martial artists compete and display their skill.

As with other aspects of kung fu, the level of participation in public demonstrations and competitions varies from school to school. As a rule, wushu schools will be more involved in such things than kung fu schools because the wushu forms have been devised specifically for those purposes (see chapter 3: "Styles"). At larger schools with many young people, tournaments may be the highlights of the year, and most, if not all, students eagerly participate. Schools located near large and thriving Chinese communities are likely to be called on to perform lion dances throughout the year, and especially at Chinese New Year. Like tournaments, these opportunities interest a certain portion of students. In contrast, at smaller schools with older students, there may be little interest in either tournaments or public demonstrations. Nevertheless, all schools usually offer students the opportunity to participate in at least one

To Perform or Not to Perform?

Whether a school is active in giving public demonstrations or participating in competitions may be one factor for you to consider when choosing a school.

tournament or demonstration during the year. There is much to be gained from such occasions, and the following tips should help the beginner know what to expect.

Lion Dances

The lion dance is a traditional Chinese ritual of blessing for grand openings (such as the opening of a restaurant, business, festival, or store), for weddings, and for any business at Chinese New Year. There are two styles: northern and southern. They differ in the appearance of the lion costume, the style of the dance, and who performs it. In both cases the "lion" is a huge, stylized, and brightly decorated head made of bamboo and paper-mâché, carried and manipulated by one performer, while a second follows, holding up the lion's colorful cloth tail. Both are covered by the costume, with only their legs exposed; they work together to imitate an animal's movement. Northern lion dances are performed by specific organizations specializing in this art; their lions look like large playful, shaggy dogs, and their dances are more circus-like, seeking to imitate the animal's natural movements. In contrast, southern lion dances are usually performed by schools of southern styles of kung fu; their lion heads are less shaggy, and their dances have a stronger component of martial arts techniques. (Wushu schools generally do not perform lion dances.)

Southern-style lion dancing is surprisingly strenuous, and much practice must go into the coordination of head and tail. The performer in the head is usually lighter in stature, while the performer in the tail must be stronger, as

The southern-style lion dance is a dramatic display, requiring strength, endurance, and coordination—in other words, excellent kung fu skills.

he often lifts and supports the head-performer to jump up onto his shoulders or other objects. Meanwhile, the performer in the head operates the eyes, ears, and mouth, while moving the whole head (which weighs fifteen to twenty pounds) to and fro and up and down. Both performers must display excellent kung fu skills, while at the same time making the lion come alive in the performance, imitating such movements as eating, scratching, stretching, running, jumping, and playing.

Meanwhile, off to the side, there is usually a band of three musicians (also from the kung fu school) playing a large drum, cymbals, and a gong. The drummer is the leader, representing the "tiger's roar," so the lion as well as the other members of the band take their cues from its beat.

Thus, any kung fu school specializing in southern styles of kung fu—especially schools located near thriving Chinese communities—may also have a lion dance team. Students of such schools will have the opportunity to participate, and training for the lion dance is considered an excellent way to practice and improve one's kung fu skills. Performance is an honor and a privilege, but also a responsibility. Each school will have its own protocol for selecting members of the lion dance troupe.

Competitions

Kung fu and wushu tournaments vary in size and breadth. The larger ones cover a variety of kung fu styles and draw participants from a wide geographical area. The smaller tournaments may be only for a particular style or for a small geographical area. Nevertheless, they do share certain characteristics.

Events

Just as other athletic competitions are divided into events, so kung fu tournaments are similarly divided. The common events listings are:

✦ Open-hand forms (forms without weapons; these are what the beginner learns first)

✦ Short-weapon forms (forms that involve the use of small weapons, such as daggers)

✦ Long-weapon forms (forms that use the staff, spear, saber, long sword, and the like)

✦ Contact (free-sparring, in which competitors apply what they have learned in a spontaneous encounter with an opponent)

In addition, there may be events for tai chi chuan, depending on the style of kung fu.

At larger tournaments, each section might be broken down into specific forms, or there might be a few sections for the most popular forms, and then a catchall category for the rest.

Categories

Within each event, there will be categories for persons of different genders, ages, and levels of experience. The size of the tournament will often determine how finely divided these categories are. Larger tournaments will tend to have more categories, while at smaller tournaments more different kinds of people will be competing together. At an average-sized tournament, typical age categories would be seven and under, eight to twelve, thirteen to seventeen, eighteen to thirty-five, and over thirty-five (senior). Typical experience categories would be under two years (novice), two to four years (intermediate), and more than four years (advanced). Similarly, the size of the tournament will determine whether or not events are restricted to specific forms. That is, at a large tournament with many competitors, each named form may have its own event, while at a small tournament all northern-style hand forms (for example) might be grouped together.

Awards

In addition to prizes/awards/certificates/trophies for individual events, many kung fu and wushu competitions will also have a "grand champion" type of award. This goes to the person who excels in the entire breadth of kung fu forms. Specifically, this means earning the highest cumulative number of points, or highest average, in at least one event from each of the main event categories.

Entering

For any competition or tournament, registration forms and descriptions usually go out well before the date of the event—that is, six months to a year in advance. Generally, the sifu of the school will decide which tournaments the school will participate in, according to the school's style or philosophy, and will post descriptive information and entrance forms somewhere in the school. Often, too, the sifu will invite specific students to participate in certain events, based on his or her assessment of their skill and accomplishment. This is a matter of both protocol and good sense. When you compete, you will be representing your school, and you don't want to embarrass yourself, your sifu, or your fellow students in the school. If you would like to participate but haven't been invited, the best strategy might be to bring the matter up with a senior instructor. Similarly, if you hear of a tournament that interests you but that your school is not going to participate in, feel free to go watch. But before you register to compete, it would be best to ask or at least inform your sifu.

By Invitation Only

Usually the sifu decides which tournaments the school joins and who will participate. As the old saying goes, let him call you, you should not call him, especially in your early years at a school.

A fee for registration is usually required, averaging thirty-five to forty dollars for the first event, with a small additional charge for each additional event. Often, too, a medical disclaimer will need to be signed, absolving the organizer of any responsibility for injuries during the tournament.

Preparing for Competition

First, do your homework. Read the rules of the tournament even before you enter, and be sure you understand them thoroughly, especially as they apply to the events you will participate in. If you have any questions, ask an instructor before the tournament, not after you get there. Talk to other students who have attended tournaments, especially this particular tournament. Practice often in front of an audience, as you will have to do at the tournament. Prepare yourself for the fact that things may not go smoothly and may not go the way you expect. For instance, tournaments often start late, and events get behind; sometimes categories are combined because too few competitors have shown up (that is, you may end up competing against people older or younger than you). One very important consideration, often overlooked by first-time competitors, is that the floor of the tournament venue is likely to be different from the one you are used to. Some tournaments are held on hardwood gym floors, some on carpet, some on mats. This will greatly affect your footwork—

Prepare for the worst—then you won't be disappointed!

so if you have the chance to try out your form on different surfaces, do it. It is practice well worth your time.

Finally, on the day of the tournament, arrive on time in a clean uniform, well rested, well nourished, and well hydrated. Bring a supply of water (and food if you think you will need it).

At the Tournament

Once you have arrived, register. Then become familiar with the venue—find the restrooms, water fountains, and doors. In addition there should be a warming-up area and an area where performers wait to be called. Be sure you know where you should be and at what time. Then spend time before the tournament thoroughly warming up—the routine and vigor of the warm-up should help to settle your nerves while preparing your body for performance.

Tournaments usually begin with an opening ceremony, at which the most senior sifus will say a few words of welcome and encouragement. Then competitions will proceed simultaneously in different areas of the tournament

If you know anyone who has been to the tournament in previous years, ask him or her for details of how things go. The fewer the surprises, the greater your confidence.

venue—much like the different rings of a circus. Usually there will be several judges for each event; the number will vary according to the size of the tournament and the school. In some cases, one judge might sit at each of the four corners of the performance area, ensuring coverage from all angles for assigning scores. In a typical competition, each performer will be called by name to perform. He or she will enter the ring, stand before the head judge, bow and/ or give the school's salute, and then perform. At the end of the performance, scores will be given—sometimes announced. After all competitors in that particular category have performed, all may be called back to stand at attention before the head judge. The winners will then be announced; competitors bow and disperse. In case of a tie, the competitors may be asked to perform again. In addition, the scores from the individual events will be used to determine the grand champion, as described above.

Performance Criteria

For both public performances and competitions, a number of aspects of performance are considered important that might not be relevant to school practice or to simply mastering the forms. To know the criteria and expectations for any specific competition, you have two sources of information: First, thoroughly read the rules and guidelines. Second, ask those who have competed before and heed their advice carefully. A voice or two of experience can help you tremendously.

Specifics aside, in general the following are the kind of criteria that judges will use to evaluate performances.

Physical Space

Stay within the perimeter of the space allotted for performance; if you go beyond, points are deducted. Usually the space will be clearly marked with tape or lines and will be generous. Having practiced your form many times before, you should know where to start so as to be sure to have enough room in critical directions.

If appropriate for the form you are doing, finish as close as possible to the exact spot where you started. Interestingly, many forms are intended to begin and end in the same place.

Time Limit

Respect the time limit. Going over the time limit will cost you points; even worse, it shows disrespect to the other performers, the judges, and the audience.

The Form

Follow the exact sequence of movements as specified—either according to tradition or according to recent specifications (wushu).

Perform each movement accurately. Do not slur. That is, finish each movement neatly, cleanly, and completely before beginning the next. (Sloppiness often creeps in when nervousness causes a performer to speed up.)

Performance

Speed

Timing

Coordination (especially of upper/lower body and hands/feet)

Power

Endurance

Balance

Agility

Alertness (facial expression, eye movement/position)

Crispness

Demonstrations

Aside from competitions and tournaments, some kung fu schools are asked to give demonstrations of their art at public events, such as festivals and school fairs. Whether performing individually or as part of a group, you should prepare for such demonstrations in much the same way as you prepare for competition. Learn as much as you can about where you will be performing, and then practice. Arrive on the appointed day well rested, on time, with a clean uniform. Remind yourself that you are representing your school and the art of kung fu, so that you will behave and perform with respect and dignity.

Mental Attitude

To some kung fu masters and enthusiasts, performances and competitions seem to degrade and trivialize a very serious art. After all, in its original context, kung fu combat was to the death, and most of the treasured secrets were how to kill or seriously, if not permanently, injure an opponent. Nevertheless there is value in performance for most modern students.

First, performing in front of any kind of audience will help you develop concentration. Being able to do the form well is the first step; then you must be able to do it well, consistently, under all kinds of conditions.

Second, performance highlights the finality of what we are doing—in performance as in life itself. In most cases you have no second chance: you must

Making mistakes could help you more than winning.

start, and then finish. You must ignore watching eyes, you must ignore what you've seen of other competitors (good or bad), and you must not let any of that interfere with your concentration or your determination to do your best. Performance challenges you not only with the specter of making a mistake but also with the grim reality of having to carry on after you have made the mistake. Ironically, the most valuable performance is perhaps not one in which you perform flawlessly, but rather one in which you do make an error and then must recover and continue to try your best. You must not let a momentary failure

interfere with the rest of your performance; instead, you must reapply your
concentration with renewed determination, lest your mistakes multiply.

Third, performance and competition
remind you that, when you perform,
you represent not only yourself, but also
every group to which you belong—your

> Use the competition as
> an opportunity to renew
> your motivation and vision of
> what you want to achieve,
> as well as a reality check on
> what you have achieved.

family, your school, your style of kung fu, even your state or nation at the
higher levels of competition. Dedicated effort, respectful behavior, as well as
accomplished kung fu, all bring honor to those with whom you are associated.
Your parents, your sifu, your fellow students, your friends: all will feel proud
when you perform well.

Fourth, participating in a tournament or public demonstration gives you the
chance to learn from others: to receive inspiration as well as ideas and hints
on how to improve your own technique. Like the freshness of a summer
breeze, seeing others can revitalize your practice and renew your enthusiasm.
Meeting others can grow into new friendships and strengthen your ties to the
kung fu community.

Finally, competition should remind you that the most important measuring
of how well or how badly you do is within yourself, not in any judge's seat. In
other words, if you compete, do not take the outcome too seriously. Remember
that how you place will be influenced by factors other than simply how you
performed. The quality of the judges and the other performers will also influence how you score. Remember that there is no "best" in any art; there are only
opinions. Remember that how much you have improved may be a better indication of your progress than what level you achieve—and there is no way for
the judges to give a score for that.

Winning Every Time

Consider any competition or performance as an opportunity to share your
accomplishments, to expose your weaknesses, to learn from others, and to find
inspiration. Continue to develop your own sense of what is good and bad. No
matter how well or poorly you performed, go home determined to do better.

On the Practice of Kung fu

THERE ARE LITERALLY HUNDREDS of books on kung fu and the martial arts; there are also magazines, videos (instructional, documentary, and entertainment), and Web sites. You will find some of these resources in your local library; you will find more in bookstores and at martial arts stores. And you will certainly find many sites on the Internet, put up both by individuals and martial arts organizations. Some sources are specific, about particular styles or masters; others (particularly the magazines) are general, covering the whole range of Asian martial arts. Some focus on technique; others describe theory and background.

Because of this diversity, recommending specific reading material is beyond the scope of this book. Instead, here are three suggestions to guide your pursuit of further knowledge.

First, start by studying specifically what you are learning. If you are learning Hung Gar style, then search the Web, bookstores, and your library for information about this particular style. You may ask your sifu or the instructors for recommendations; the school may even have a library of books and magazine articles that you can borrow. Watch videos; visit Web sites. Later, as your interests expand, follow them—and feed them with as much (or as little) information as you want.

Second, read everything. Try not to think in terms of what is good or bad, but rather try to be open to everyone's interpretation and understanding. This is especially sound advice for beginners, because those new to a discipline don't have enough experience to judge. What seems good now—what attracts you now—may not seem at all valuable to you later. So read widely and indiscriminately. But, at the same time, always consider ideas for yourself, testing them against your own experience. In this way, you will learn something from everything you see or read, and you will develop a broad, balanced, and sound understanding.

Third, keep in mind that the goal is not to become a walking encyclopedia; rather, the goal is to develop your own sense of what the art of kung fu is all about and how to do it. As in eating, where the goal of digestion is to transform food into energy and discard waste, so your goal should be to listen, learn, and then internalize only what you find useful. Also, remember that reading and watching videos can support your training, but never replace it—just as reading a menu can never fill your stomach.

In the *Tao Te Ching*, it is written:

> In order to learn, you must daily accumulate.
> In order to follow the Way of the Tao, you must daily eliminate.

So it is with kung fu. In the first stage, accumulate knowledge. In the second stage, digest the knowledge, making it your own. And in the third stage, forget all that you have learned, and simply use what has become part of you.

On the Philosophical Roots of Kung fu

To understand the philosophy that underpins the ethics of kung fu, it would be helpful to read something about Taoism, Confucianism, and Buddhism. There are many good resources—and more appear every year—of which we can recommend the following:

On Taoism, the basic primary reference is the *Tao Te Ching* by Lao-tzu. There are many translations, all of which will serve your purposes. One of the most highly respected is that by Gia-Fu Feng and Jane English (*Tao Te Ching by Lao Tsu, A New Translation*. New York: Random House, 1972).

On Buddhism, a good introduction is *What the Buddha Taught* by Walpola Sri Rahula (New York: Grove Press, 1974), although, again, there are many contemporary works, both short and long, that will cover the basic ideas of Buddhism.

On Confucianism, look for translations of *The Analects*, which is the name by which the collected sayings of Confucius are known. Lin Yutang is one of the most respected and readable authors on the subject. (Lin Yutang, ed. and trans. *Wisdom of Confucius*. New York: Modern Library, 1938.) A more modern version is a translation by Simon Leys. (Leys, Simon, trans. *The Analects of Confucius*. New York: W. W. Norton, 1997.)

The Historical and Literary Lore of Kung fu

Yet another area of essential background reading is the classical epic literature of the early dynasties of China. Two immediately come to mind. The first is *Romance of the Three Kingdoms* or simply *The Three Kingdoms* (attributed to Luo Guanzhong), which has been compared to the epics of Homer in scale and importance. Perhaps the best English translation is *The Three Kingdoms: China's Epic Drama* by Lo Kuan-chung, translated from the Chinese and edited by Moss Roberts (New York: Pantheon Books, 1976). This book is also the basis of a video game for Playstation 2, entitled *Dynasty Warriors*. The name of the second classic is roughly translated from the Chinese as "outlaws of the marsh." There are two English versions: *Water Margin*, written by Shih Nai-an, translated by J. H. Jackson (Hong Kong: Commercial Press, 1975) and an abridged but more readable version entitled *All Men Are Brothers* by Shui Hu Chuan, translated by Pearl S. Buck (New York: Grove Press, 1957). These books comprise stories of martial arts heroes and offer a glimpse of the role of martial arts in the early dynasties of China.

Finally, to learn more about the "patron saint" of the martial arts, himself a legendary hero of *The Three Kingdoms*, Guan Gung (or Guan Dai, Guan Ti), you may look for entries in books on Chinese culture, such as *Myths and Legends of China* by E.T.C. Werner (New York: Dover, 1994 reprint of a 1992 edition, published by G.G. Harrap & Co., London). Here he is called the God of War, Kuan Ti. The exploits of Kuan Ti are also included in *The Romance of the Three Kingdoms*.

Some martial arts Web sites include information, especially in relation to the weapon, the "Kwan Do," which refers to the sword (dao) of General Kwan. http://ezine.kungfumagazine.com is one resource to check.

PAUL ENG has been deeply involved in Chinese martial arts since he began his formal training in Hong Kong at the age of six. Since that time, he has studied with many noted masters both in this country and in Asia, and has himself taught for more than forty years.

Sifu Eng came to the U.S. in 1949, first living in New York, where he was Chief Instructor of the Fu Jow Pai Kung-Fu Federation, and later in San Francisco. In 1967 he entered the U.S. Army and served in Vietnam from 1967 to 1969. During this time, he continued to teach kung fu as Chief Instructor of the "Red Catcher" Combat Ranger training camp at Long Binh, of the 2nd Battalion, 3rd Infantry, 199th Infantry Brigade, and of the Military Police Battalion at Choloon. While in Vietnam, Sifu Eng also took the opportunity to study with the respected Praying Mantis Sifu Chiu Chuk Kai, first in Saigon and later in Hong Kong.

Upon returning from Vietnam, Sifu Eng, together with Raymond Wong and Kam Yuen, formed the Tai Mantis Kung-Fu Association. Since that time, Sifu Eng has operated Tai Mantis schools in San Jose, Palo Alto, and now in Campbell, California. He has taught at many schools, colleges, YMCAs, and community centers in the Bay Area and has taught tai chi chuan at the Kaiser Hospital Physical Therapy Department in Santa Clara.

Sifu Eng's background includes study with the following masters:

✦ Chin King Woon (Hong Kong)—Choi Lee Fut style

✦ Leung Hung (NY)—Tai chi chuan

✦ Chan Kwong Ming (NY)—Choi Ga style

✦ Wong Moon Toy (NY)—Fu Jow Pai (Tiger Claw System); Northern Mi Zong (Lost Track Style); Hung Garr Tiger Crane System

+ Wong Jack Man (SF)—Tai chi chuan, Hsing-I, Pa Kua, Northern Shaolin, Shaolin Lo Han
+ Chiu Chuk Kai (Saigon, HK)—Tai Chi Praying Mantis
+ Kam Yuen (LA)—Seven Star Praying Mantis

His website, www.taimantiskungfu.com, gives more details about his school's activities and other publications.